The Technical Centre for Agricultural and Rural Co-operation (CTA) operates under the Lomé Convention between member States of the European Community and the African, Caribbean and Pacific (ACP) States.

The aim of CTA is to collect, disseminate and facilitate the exchange of information on research, training and innovations in the spheres of agricultural and rural development and extension for the benefit of the ACP States.

Headquarters: 'De Rietkampen', Galvanistraat 9, Ede, Netherlands
Postal address: Postbus 380, 6700 AJ Wageningen, Netherlands
Tel: (31)(0)(8380)–60400
Telex: (44)–30169 CTA NL
Telefax: (31)(0)(8380)–31052

Agency for Cultural and Technical Co-operation (ACCT)

The Agency for Cultural and Technical Co-operation, an intergovernmental organisation set up by the Treaty of Niamey in March 1970, is an association of countries linked by their common usage of the French language, for the purposes of co-operation in the fields of education, culture, science and technology and, more generally, in all matters which contribute to the development of its Member States and to bringing peoples closer together.

The Agency's activities in the fields of scientific and technical co-operation for development are directed primarily towards the preparation, dissemination and exchange of scientific and technical information, drawing up an inventory of and exploiting natural resources, and the socio-economic advancement of young people and rural communities.

Member countries: Belgium, Benin, Burundi, Canada, Central African Republic, Chad, Comoros, Congo, Djibouti, Dominica, France, Gabon, Guinea, Haiti, Ivory Coast, Lebanon, Luxembourg, Mali, Mauritius, Monaco, Niger, Rwanda, Senegal, Seychelles, Togo, Tunisia, Burkina Faso, Vanuatu, Vietnam, Zaire.

Associated States: Cameroon, Egypt, Guinea-Bissau, Laos, Mauritania, Morocco, St Lucia.

Participating governments: New Brunswick, Quebec.

Titles in *The Tropical Agriculturalist* series (*co-published in French by Maisonneuve et Larose*)

Sheep	0–333–52310–5	Poultry	0–333–52306–7
Pigs	0–333–52308–3	Rabbits	0–333–52311–3
Goats	0–333–52309–1	Draught Animals	0–333–52307–5
Dairying	0–333–52313–X	Ruminant Nutrition	0–333–57073–1
Animal Breeding	0–333–57907–0		
		Sugar Cane	0–333–57075–8
Upland Rice	0–333–44889–8	Maize	0–333–44404–3
Tea	0–333–54450–1	Plantain Bananas	0–333–44813–8
Cotton	0–333–47280–2	Coffee Growing	0–333–54451–X
Weed Control	0–333–54449–8	Food Legumes	0–333–53850–1
Spice Plants	0–333–57460–5	Cassava	0–333–47395–7
Cocoa	0–333–57076–6	Sorghum	0–333–54452–8
The Storage of Food Grains and Seeds	0–333–44827–8		

Other titles published by Macmillan with CTA (*co-published in French by Maisonneuve et Larose*)

Animal Production in the Tropics and SubTropics	0–333–53818–8
Coffee: The Plant and the Product	0–333–57296–3
The Tropical Vegetable Garden	0–333–57077–4
Controlling Crop Pests and Diseases	0–333–57216–5
Dryland Farming in Africa	0–333–47654–9
The Yam	0–333–57456–7

The Land and Life Series (*co-published with Terres et Vie*)

African Gardens and Orchards	0–333–49076–2
Vanishing Land and Water	0–333–44597–X
Ways of Water	0–333–57078–2
Agriculture in African Rural Communities	0–333–44595–3

Contents

Preface

Most people are not particularly interested in agriculture, but spices arouse a fascination which goes well beyond their economic importance. This special status, which spice plants in general enjoy, is even more pronounced for spices of tropical origin. There is something subconsciously exciting about the flavours and aromas of these foodstuffs, enhanced even more by their names; cinnamon, cloves, cardamom, allspice, the sounds of which conjure up the traditional and conventional images of the tropics: blue skies, sunshine, idleness and daydreams.

Many people also have a dim recollection from school of the caravans of the Middle Ages, the travels of Marco Polo or a poem about the conquistadors setting off in ships to discover America. In short, an aura of legend and poetry surrounds spice production and trade, something which cereal or root vegetable production simply does not evoke.

The agronomist, however, is obliged to come down to earth to the botany and cultivation of these plants, which are precise disciplines but which nevertheless also have their attractions.

It is in this spirit, indeed that of the series of which this volume is a part, that we have attempted to deal with a subject which cannot be covered in a few pages.

The task was greatly simplified by the support afforded by the key work written by J. Maistre (1905–1981), entitled *Spice plants* (III. Techniques Agricoles et Productions Tropicales. Maisonneuve & Larose). This manual, which was published a quarter of a century ago, is still an indispensable source of reference on the subject and the only one in French. It is unfortunately out of print and a new run is not planned.

It is hoped that the present manual, which is more concise and slightly different in content, being directed at a wider readership, will partly fill the current gap. In so doing, we would like to pay homage to our colleague and predecessor at the head of the Aromatic Plant Department at the IRAT.

M. Borget

1 General information

Without going into too many details on points of vocabulary or nomenclature, two terms which relate to substances added in small quantities to food, in order to modify the flavour of the food, need to be defined.

Spice: 'A vegetable substance of indigenous or exotic origin which is aromatic or has a hot, piquant taste, used to enhance the flavour of foods or to add to them the stimulant ingredients contained in them. (Definition adopted at the first International Conference on the Repression of Fraud. Geneva, 1980.)

Condiment: Substance which is added to food to enhance its flavour. Salt is the most common of the condiments.

This general definition differs little from that of **seasoning**. For the purposes of this book, it is important to remember that the term 'spice' refers to a substance: 1) of vegetable origin, 2) coming from a single defined botanical species. Pepper is a **spice**. Mustard, however, which is made up of ground mustard seeds, vinegar and salt, is a **condiment**.

1.1 *History*

The use of spices and condiments, and of salt in particular, dates back to ancient times. Archaeological excavations have revealed that prehistoric man used the leaves of certain plants to enhance the flavour of the half-cooked foods which he ate. Spices are mentioned in the Bible. Ancient Greeks and Romans were familiar with spices, and paid high prices for them.

The conquests of Alexander the Great increased this taste for oriental spices which was also shared by other invaders. In 410 AD, Alaric, king of the Visigoths, who was threatening to sack Rome, demanded that among other riches, Rome give him 3000 pounds of pepper!

Throughout the Middle Ages, the spice trade was in the hands of Arab traders, who began operating around 1000 years BC. Their caravans brought the spices from the Orient to Cairo or Alexandria, where they were bought by Genoan and Venetian traders who transported them to Europe. Here they were resold at very high prices. This virtual monopoly of the Arab caravan drivers was carefully guarded by the interested parties and by their Venetian counterparts, preserving legends and fables surrounding the mysterious origins of these foodstuffs.

However, as the state of knowledge was advanced by the experiences of the first great explorers, the most famous being that of Marco Polo in 1721, more and more people learned about spices and wanted to take advantage of this lucrative trade, bypassing the traditional routes. There then followed fierce competition between those European nations which had an active commercial fleet, which was to last several centuries.

The Portuguese navigators were first on the scene. At the beginning of the 16th century, a large cargo of spices was taken from the Moluccan archipelago by a Portuguese navigator. Others followed, thus earning the Kingdom of Portugal a much-envied supremacy in this trade. Spain disliked this situation and it became one of the reasons behind the financing of the expeditions of Christopher Columbus. The initial aim was to reach the Indies by going West in search of 'gold and spices' and the discovery of the West Indies and of the American continent was, in a way, fortuitous. Unfortunately, these lands had very few spice plants, the vast majority of which originated in Asia.

The Dutch broke the Portuguese hold on the Far East by conquering Malacca and Sumatra in the middle of the 18th century. By the end of that century they controlled virtually all of the islands which today make up Indonesia. For some time they were masters of the spice trade with a very protectionist policy which involved monitoring crop extension, destroying stocks which were too large and prohibiting all traffic in seeds.

However, during the early 1800s, monopoly crumbled under the influence of the English who had taken hold in India and who, up to the mid 1800s, played a major role in the trade in these products.

As time went on, these foodstuffs became more abundant as crops were extended, first in the countries of origin, then in other countries. Prices fell and less wealthy consumers were able to purchase spices, which were gradually becoming less thought of as luxury items, a status held for more than four centuries. Nowadays, although often still surrounded by speculation, the spice trade resembles any other trade in agricultural products.

France has played a small role in the expansion of the spice trade. Pierre Poivre (1719–1786) despite fierce opposition from the Dutch, successfully brought clove, cinnamon and nutmeg plants to the Ile de France from the Dutch Indies. From that time, it was possible to propagate these plants on the neighbouring islands and even as far as Guyana. It was the first breach in Dutch protectionism.

1.2 The most commonly used spices

The list of spices in Table 1, which does not claim to be an exhaustive list of all the plants in this category, is composed only of cultivated plants. Indigenous species which are harvested are therefore not included. The tropical species are in bold print.

Table 1 *Common spices*

Common name	French name	Botanical name	Family
Allspice/ Pimento	**Piment de la Jamaique**	*Pimenta dioica*	Myrtaceae
Angelica	Angelique	*Angelica archangelica*	Umbelliferae
Anise	Anis vert	*Pimpinella anisum*	Umbelliferae
Basil	Basilic	*Ocimum basilicum*	Umbelliferae
Bay laurel	Laurier	*Laurus nobilis*	Lauraceae
Black pepper	**Poivrier**	*Piper nigrum*	Piperaceae
Caper	Capre	*Capparis spinosa*	Capparidaceae
Caraway	Carvi	*Carum carvi*	Umbelliferae
Cardamom	**Cardamome**	*Elettaria cardamomum*	Zingiberaceae
Cassia	**Cannelles autres**	*Cinnamomum divers*	Lauraceae
Celery	Celeri	*Apium graviolens*	Umbelliferae
Chervil	Cerfeuil	*Anthriscus cerefolium*	Umbelliferae
Chilli	**Piment de Cayenne**	*Capsicum frutescens*	Solanaceae
Chives	Ciboulette	*Allium schoenoprasum*	Liliaceae
Cinnamon	**Cannelle vraie**	*Cinnamomum verum*	Lauraceae
Clove	**Giroflier**	*Syzygium aromaticum*	Myrtaceae
Coriander	Coriandre	*Coriandrum sativum*	Umbelliferae
Cumin	Cumin	*Cuminum cyminum*	Umbelliferae
Dill	Aneth	*Anethum graveolens*	Umbelliferae

Common name	French name	Botanical name	Family
Fennel	Fenouil	*Foeniculum vulgare*	Umbelliferae
Fenugreek	Fenugrec	*Trigonella foenum-graecum*	Papilionaceae
Galangal	**Alpinie**	*Alpinia officinarum*	Zingiberaceae
Garlic	Ail	*Allium sativum*	Liliaceae
Gherkin	Cornichon	*Cucumis sativus*	Cucurbitaceae
Ginger	**Gingembre**	*Zingiber officinale*	Zingiberaceae
Horseradish	Raifort	*Armoracia rusticana*	Cruciferae
Juniper	Genevrier	*Juniperus communis*	Cupressaceae
Lemon grass	**Citronelle**	*Cymbopogon citratus*	Graminaceae
Marjoram	Origan	*Origanum majorana*	Labiatae/ Lamiaceae
Melegueta pepper	**Maniguette**	*Aframomum melegueta*	Zingiberaceae
Mint	Menthes	*Mentha viridis*	Labiatae/ Lamiaceae
Mustard	Moutarde	*Brassica nigra*	Cruciferae
Nutmeg	**Muscadier**	*Myristica fragrans*	Myristicaceae
Onion	Oignon	*Allium cepa*	Liliaceae
Parsley	Persil	*Petroselinum sativum*	Umbelliferae
Pepper	Piment	*Capsicum annuum*	Solanaceae
Rosemary	Romarin	*Rosmarinus officinalis*	Labiatae/ Lamiaceae
Saffron	Safran	*Crocus sativus*	Iridaceae
Sage	Sauge	*Salvia officinalis*	Labiatae/ Lamiaceae
Savory	Sarriette	*Satureia hortensis*	Labiatae/ Lamiaceae
Sassafras	Sassafras	*Sassafras officinalis*	Lauraceae
Spring onion	Ciboule	*Allium fistulosum*	Liliaceae
Star anise	Badiane	*Illicium verum*	Illiciaceae
Tamarind	**Tamarin**	*Tamarindus indica*	Caesalpiniaceae
Tarragon	Estragon	*Artemisia dracunculus*	Compositae
Thyme	Thym	*Thymus vulgaris*	Labiatae/ Lamiaceae
Turmeric	**Curcuma**	*Curcuma domestica*	Zingiberaceae
Vanilla	**Vanille**	*Vanilla fragrans*	Orchidaceae
Welsh onion	Civette	*Allium fistulosum*	Liliaceae

1.3 *Species studied in detail*

Given the limited space available in this book, it was not possible to study all the tropical spice species listed above. It was therefore necessary to make a choice, which is always difficult, and open to criticism. The following criteria were selected and adhered to:

- a detailed study of the species which are the most important economically and which, for this reason, appear in production and consumption statistics;
- as faithful a picture as possible of the range of growing conditions, due to the diversity of biological types: trees, vines and rhizomatous plants;
- an account of all the different plant-parts used, i.e. bark, rhizomes, leaves, flower buds, fruits and seeds;
- a detailed study of the species originating in the three continents with large tropical zones, namely Asia, America and Africa. Africa does not have large numbers of spice plants but there was a considerable trade in Melegueta pepper at the beginning of this century. It therefore appears in the list of species studied in detail;
- the term 'tropical' regarding only those species which actually originate in tropical regions, and are not cultivated elsewhere. For this reason peppers (*Capsicum annuum*), an important species in the tropics, do not appear in this book because they are also extensively grown in countries with a temperate climate.

Listed below in Table 2 are the ten species which will be studied in detail:

Table 2 *Species studied in detail*

Common name	Type	Continent of origin	Part used
Pepper	Vine	Asia	Whole fruits and seeds
Vanilla	Vine	America	Whole fruits
Cinnamon	Tree	Asia	Bark and leaves
Nutmeg	Tree	Asia	Seeds and arils
Cloves	Tree	Asia	Flower buds, hypanthia and leaves
Allspice	Tree	America	Whole fruits and leaves
Ginger	Rhizome	Asia	Rhizomes
Turmeric	Rhizome	Asia	Rhizomes
Cardamom	Rhizome	Asia	Seeds
Melegueta pepper	Rhizome	Africa	Seeds

1.4 Production statistics

Spice production has not been fully dealt with in recent statistics, except for pepper, vanilla, cloves and ginger, which are listed in Table 5.

Table 4 (pages 8 and 9) gives an average production figure calculated over the years 1975 to 1985 and is only an indicator of orders of magnitude. It also shows the producing countries. Figures in bold print correspond to the country with the highest production of each species; dashes indicate production of less than 100 tonnes per annum.

This summary of the production of whole spices must be accompanied by some details of the production of the extracts, essential oils and oleoresins, about which more detailed information will be given in Chapter 4. It should be pointed out that for three of the spices studied, namely cinnamon, cloves and allspice, the essential oil can be extracted either from the spice itself or from the leaves of the tree. Furthermore, the products involved have widely-differing characteristics.

Table 3 *Production of essential oils and oleoresins from spices throughout the world*

Products	Producing countries	Tonnes/year
Essential oils		
Pepper	India, Indonesia, USA, United Kingdom	25–35
Cinnamon (leaves)	Sri Lanka	100
Cinnamon (bark)	Sri Lanka	1
Allspice (berries)	Jamaica	5
Allspice (leaves)	Jamaica	30–45
Cloves (leaves)	Madagascar, Indonesia	1 800
Cloves (heads)	Madagascar, Sri Lanka, Brazil	40–50
Cloves (hypanthia)	Tanzania (Zanzibar)	declining
Nutmeg	Indonesia, Sri Lanka	100–130
Mace	Grenada	little
Ginger	India, China	10–20
Cardamom	India, Sri Lanka, Guatemala	10–20
Oleoresins		
Pepper	India, Singapore, USA, Canada, Indonesia	400
Cloves	USA, United Kingdom	15
Nutmeg	USA, United Kingdom, Canada, Singapore	75–100
Ginger	USA, India, Singapore, Indonesia	150
Turmeric	USA, western Europe, India	100

Without precise statistics, the figures given can only be indicative. They come from a market survey of these products carried out by the Centre for International Commerce (CNUCED/GATT) in Geneva.

Table 5 *Annual production, in tonnes, of the most important spices. (Average over 1985, 1986 and 1987 for pepper and vanilla; over 1987–88 for ginger and cloves)*

	India	Indonesia	Malaysia	Brazil	Madagascar	Comoro Islands	Reunion	Tanzania
Pepper	33 990	28 600	16 150	24 510	2 100			
Vanilla		297			846	167	21	
Ginger	15 000	27 260						
Cloves				3 000	8 000	600		6 000

(Source: FAO and tropical markets.)

Table 4 *Spice-producing countries. Annual production (1000 tonnes) (Dashes indicate production of less than 100 tonnes/year)*

Country	Species									
	Pepper	Vanilla	Cinnamon	Nutmeg	Clove	Allspice	Ginger	Turmeric	Cardamom	Melegueta pepper
Asia										
India	**30**						14	**10.1**	**1.8**	
Pakistan								0.4	0.2	
Sri Lanka	2	**0.3**	5.5	0.1	**2**		4	–	–	
Thailand	8	–					–			
Indonesia	27			**5**			27			
Malaysia	20						–			
Taiwan							6	0.3		
Hong Kong							–			
Oceania										
Tahiti										
Australia							–			
Fiji										
America										
Brazil	**28**				**3**					
Peru							–	–		

	C1	C2	C3	C4	C5	C6	C7	C8	C9	C10
Mexico										—
Honduras										
Guatemala									**0.6**	
El Salvador									—	
Costa Rica									—	
Haiti									—	
Grenada						1.0				
Trinidad						0.1				
Jamaica				**1.6**		0.3	**4**			
Africa				—		5.5				
Sierra Leone							**4.5**			—
Cote d'Ivoire			—				3			—
Ghana										—
Nigeria							1.5			
Cameroon	—									
Uganda										
Kenya		—	—		6		—			
Tanzania		—	—		8					
Madagascar	3	**0.8**							**0.2**	
Reunion		—						**0.5**		
Seychelles		0.15	0.2		0.6					
Comoro Is.										
World total	119	1.3	7	7	20	7	65	11.5	3	—

9

2 Botany and ecology

2.1 *Botanical and common names*

Each species of spice plant studied has a Latin botanical name and one
or more common names. The main ones are listed in Table 6, with
common names in English and French. These are general names describing the whole plant or product, and not commercial terms used to describe
the various types of product or its different presentations, which will be
discussed later in Chapter 3.

There should only be one botanical name, which is the one used
internationally. This should be strictly adhered to. However, revisions of
the arrangement of a group of genera or even of a single genus occasionally lead botanists to make synonyms of botanical names used for decades,
which can sometimes be rather misleading.

For this reason, several of the names used in the book by Maistre
(1964) are no longer valid. For example:
Cinnamomum zeylanicum Garc. ex Bl. has become *C. verum* Presl.
Curcuma longa L. has become *C. domestica* Val. and
Vanilla planifolia Andr. has become *V. fragrans* (Salisb.) Ames.

It should also be noted that one of the English names of 'Piment de
la Jamaïque', 'Pimento', like its French equivalent is unfortunate because
the plant described has nothing to do with peppers (*Capsicum* sp., Solanaceae). The same is true of the term 'Safran des Indes' used to describe
turmeric. Saffron and turmeric have nothing in common from a botanical
point of view.

2.2 *Geographical origin*

It is very likely that seven of the ten species of spice plant studied in this
book have a Far Eastern origin in the Indo-Malaysian region of the
Moluccan archipelago. Two species originated in America (vanilla and
allspice) and only one originated in Africa (grains of paradise).

Many of these species have been cultivated for a long time and some

Table 6 *Botanical and common names*

Botanical name	Common name	
	English	**French**
Piper nigrum L	Black pepper	Poivrier
Vanilla fragrans (Salisb.) Ames Syn: V. planifolia Andr.	Vanilla	Vanillier
Cinnamomum verum Presl. Syn: C. zeylanicum Nees Laurus cinnamomum L.	Ceylon cinnamon	Cannelier de Ceylan
Myristica fragrans Houtt. Syn: M. officinalis L. f. M. aromatica Swarytz M. moschata Thunb.	Nutmeg tree	Muscadier
Syzygium aromaticum (L.) Merr. & Perry Syn: Caryophyllus aromatica L. Eugenia aromatica (L.) Baillon E. caryophyllus (Sprengel) Bullock & Harrison E. caryophyllata Thunb.	Clove tree	Giroflier
Pimenta dioica (L.) Merr. Syn: P. officinalis Lindl. Myrtus pimenta L. M. dioica L. Eugenia pimenta DC.	Jamaican pimento Jamaican pepper Pimento Allspice	Quatre-épices Piment de la Jamaïque
Zingiber officinale Roscoe	Ginger	Gingembre
Curcuma domestica Val. Syn: C. longa Kœnig	Turmeric Madras turmeric Haiti turmeric	Curcuma Safran des Indes
Elettaria cardamomum (L.) Maton var. minuscula Burkill	Malabar cardamom Mysore cardamom Mangalore cardamom	Cardamome de Malabar
Aframomum melegueta (Rosc.) K. Schum. Syn: Amomum melegueta Rosc.	Grains of Paradise Guinea grains Melegueta Malagueta pepper Melegueta pepper	Maniguette Graines de Paradis

are no longer recognised as wild species. In the light of the most recent research, it is possible to give the current distribution of each one of them.

Black pepper originated in India and is still found growing wild on the south western coast of this sub-continent, known as the Malabar Coast.

Cinnamon is indigenous to Sri Lanka (Ceylon, before independence), hence the botanical name *Cinnamomum zeylanicum* commonly used until recently.

Nutmeg is indigenous to the Moluccan archipelago (Amboina, Ternate and other islands), but nowadays it is very rarely found in its wild state.

The **clove** plant also originated in the Moluccan islands. There is less certainty than there used to be about the origins of **ginger** and **turmeric**, which are unknown in the wild state. These two species probably originated in India.

Cardamom also originated in India and Sri Lanka where it is found growing wild in the mountain forests.

Vanilla is indigenous to Central America (Guatemala in particular), to south-east Mexico and also to some islands in the West Indies.

Allspice is found in Central America (Guatemala, Costa Rica and Honduras), in the south of Mexico and on some of the West Indian islands (Cuba, Haiti and Jamaica).

'Melegueta pepper' or 'grains of paradise' is one of the very few spices which originated in Africa. It is found on the west coast of Africa, from Guinea to Angola. A hundred years ago there was a sizeable trade in this spice via Dieppe and Rouen.

2.3 *Detailed descriptions of the species studied*

The following descriptions are given in the form of data sheets in a single, systematic format. They are accompanied by figures which are sketches, intended to show the main points of the morphology of the plant and are not drawings of herbarium samples or of the living plant. Wherever possible, all attempts have been made to avoid the use of an over-specialised botanical vocabulary. Therefore there has been as much simplification as possible and the corresponding figures (1 to 10) will help readers to understand these descriptions.

Vines

Black pepper (*Piper nigrum* L.) – Piperaceae

Type   Perennial vine clinging to and climbing on its support by means of adventitious roots.

Root system
1. Adventitious aerial roots in a cluster at a node.
2. Shallow (30–60 cm long) underground functional roots in bundles; some main roots (6–12) penetrating the soil to a considerable depth.

Stems
1. Stolons at ground level.
2. Vertical (orthotropic) stems which carry the adventitious roots

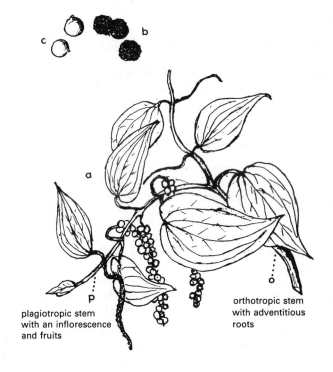

plagiotropic stem
with an inflorescence
and fruits

orthotropic stem
with adventitious
roots

a) General view
b) Black peppercorns
c) White peppercorns

Fig 1   *Black pepper plant (*Piper nigrum *L.)*

and generate the secondary (plagiotropic) branches.
Internodes 7–12 cm in length × 1–3 cm in diameter.
3. Plagiotropic stems which carry the inflorescences and are approximately horizontal.
Internodes 4–6 cm in length × 1–1.5 cm in diameter.

Leaves   Single, alternate, with stipulated petioles. Petiole length 2–3 cm; two stipules forming a sheath at their base. The leaves are oval with pointed ends, coriaceous, rounded becoming approximately heart-shaped at the base, symmetrical on the orthotropic stems, asymmetrical on the plagiotropic stems. 10–15 cm long × 5–10 cm wide. Lustrous and dark green above; paler green and matt below.

Inflorescence   Dense spike of ± 100 flowers; 7–12 cm long, arising at the node opposite the leaf.

Flower   Apetalous, unisexual or bisexual, greenish white, two to four stamens; three to five stigmata; one ovule.

Fruit   Spherical berry 0.5–0.8 cm in diameter, green, turning to yellow then red when mature; 18 300/kg (dry state = black pepper).

Seeds   Spherical, greyish white (white pepper) 0.4 cm in diameter. Weight of 1000 seeds = 33–55 g. Number of seeds/kg = 19 000–31 000.

Vanilla (*Vanilla fragrans* (Salisb.) Ames) – Orchidaceae

Type   Perennial vine clinging to and climbing on its support by means of adventitious roots.

Root system
1. Aerial, adventitious roots borne opposite the leaves, approximately 8–10 cm long × 0.2 cm in diameter.
2. Fairly shallow, underground branching roots invaded by mycorrhizae.

Stem   Dark green, glabrous, fleshy, succulent, cylindrical; 1–2 cm in diameter. Internodes up to 15 cm in length.

Leaves   Alternate subsessile, dark green, glabrous, without stipules. Short, flattened petiole, merging into the lamina. Lamina 8–25 cm × 2–8 cm, oblong, elliptical and lanceolate with a rounded base and a pointed tip. Numerous veins parallel to the main vein.

Inflorescence   Short axillary raceme, 5–8 cm long with 6 to 15 flowers. This inflorescence is called a 'broom' in Réunion.

Flowers   Large, white, perfumed, with a waxy, irregular, orchid-like

a) General view with stem and inflorescence
b) Fruit (pod) after preparation

Fig 2   *Vanilla (*Vanilla fragrans *(Salisb.) Ames)*

appearance. Three oblong sepals, 4–7 cm long × 1.5 cm wide. Three petals, two free, resembling the sepals and one rolled into a trumpet shape 4–5 cm long × 1.5 cm wide. A fertile stamen containing two pollinia, attached to the style in a column (gynostemium). Stigma protected by a thin layer forming a flap (rostellum) which isolates it from the stamen. Trilocular ovary; very small ovules, numerous inferior ovaries forming a false flower stalk.

Fruit   An elongated, pendant capsule (pod) 10–25 cm long × 0.8–1.5 cm wide. Triangular in section with rounded corners, opening longitudinally when mature. Harvesting is carried out before the fruit opens.

Seeds   Numerous black, globular, 0.3 mm in diameter.

Trees

Cinnamon (*Cinnamomum verum Presl.*) – Lauraceae

Type   Large, evergreen, heavily branching tree, with a bushy habit, 10–15 m high.

Trunk   Thick, furrowed bark, smelling and tasting of cinnamon.

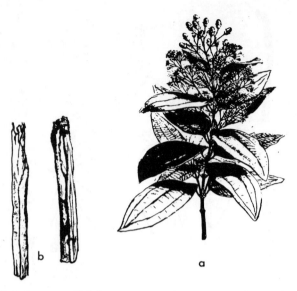

a) Tip of a flowering stem with inflorescence
   and young roots (after Baillon)
b) Bark (quills) after preparation

Fig 3 *Cinnamon (*Cinnamomum verum *Presl)*

Leaves Opposite, single, petiolated, without stipules. Petiole 1–1.3 cm long. Oblong, oval leaf, bluntly pointed, 10–18 cm long × 4–5 cm wide. Three to five characteristic longitudinal ribs running from the base to the end of the lamina. Leaves glossy, dark green above and matt, light green below. Young leaves tinged with pink.

Inflorescence Regular, loose, terminal or axillary cymes of 15 to 60 flowers.

Flowers Small, regular, yellowish white, bisexual. Six sepals; no petals; 12 stamens, 9 of which are fertile. Anther opening by four flaps. Unilocular ovary containing one ovule.

Fruit Fleshy, black, globulous drupe, containing the remains of the calyx, 1.5 cm in diameter × 2 cm long.

Seeds One ovoid seed per fruit, 1.1–1.7 cm long.

Clove (*Syzygium aromaticum* (L.) Merr. & Perry) – Myrtaceae

Type Large evergreen tree, 12–15 m high, with a naturally conical profile, branching at the base and not as tall when cultivated.

Root system Well-developed, thick mass of root hairs on the surface which provides only weak anchorage, reinforced by a number of deep, vertical roots.

Trunk   Grey, smooth bark. Small, fragile branches. Opposite primary branches, pyramidal profile.

Leaves   Opposite, single, petiolated, without stipules. Petiole 0.6–1.2 cm long, reddish. Lanceolated lamina, slim at the base, pointed at the tip, 7–13 cm long × 2.5–4 cm wide. Leaves tinged red above, dark green on the underside. Aromatic odour when bruised. Young leaves pink to copper-coloured.

Inflorescence   Cymes grouped in terminal panicles 4–5 cm long bearing 20–40 flowers. Inflorescences appearing several months before the flowers bloom.

Flowers   Regular, bisexual, tubular, pink calyx, ending with four short fleshy sepals 0.4–1 cm long. Four whitish-pink petals, forming a small dome which falls when the flower opens. Numerous stamens; bilocular ovary containing a large number of ovules. The **clove**

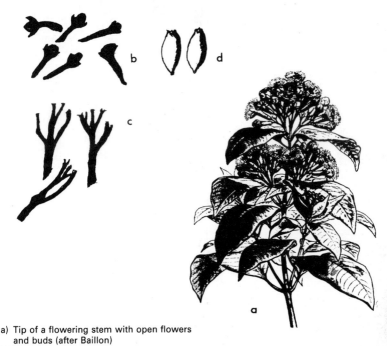

a) Tip of a flowering stem with open flowers and buds (after Baillon)
b) Cloves
c) Claws
d) Fruits

Fig 4   *Clove plant (*Syzygium aromaticum *L. Merr. & Perry)*

is the flower bud at an early stage in its development when the calyx is bright red and the corolla is still present.

Fruit Brownish purple, fleshy, ellipsoid, obovoid drupe, 2.5 cm long × 1 cm in diameter. Ripe fruit called the 'mother of cloves'. It is ripe 2–3 months after flowering.

Seeds Normally only one, oblong, 1.3–1.5 cm long. 10 000 dry cloves per litre. Weight of 1000 cloves = 35 g.

Allspice (*Pimenta dioica* (L.) Merr.) – Myrtaceae

Type Large, evergreen tree, 7–12 m high, which may grow to more than 20 m.

Trunk Relatively slender with ramified branches. Smooth, shiny, silvery bark. Young branches develop numerous quadrangular formations at the ends of the secondary branches.

a) Tip of a stem with fruits
b) Dried berries

Fig 5   *Allspice (*Pimenta dioica *L. Merr.)*

18

Leaves Single, opposite, coriaceous, petiolated, emitting an aromatic odour when bruised. Petiole 1–1.5 cm long. Lamina elliptical to oblong, 6–15 cm long × 3–6 cm wide. Dark green above, light green below.

Inflorescence Tightly-spaced cymes at the end of peduncles, 5–15 cm long.

Flowers Regular, white, perfumed, bisexual (there are plants which are functionally either male or female), 0.8–1 cm in diameter. Four sepals 1.5–2 cm long, four petals forming a crown, numerous stamens. Bilocular ovary, one ovule in each loculus. Some 'male' plants bear only a few fruits. Their flowers have a great many stamens (about 100) whereas the flowers of the 'female' plants have less (about 50).

Fruit Spherical, reddish brown when mature. 0.5 cm in diameter (approximately the size of a small pea). Harvested when green and turn black as they dry. The dried fruit is the commercial product, having a very aromatic smell.

Seeds Kidney-shaped, two per fruit, surrounded by a mucilaginous pulp, separated one from the other by a thin membrane. The fruits which are only rarely borne by the 'male' trees contain only a single seed. 1 200 to 1 300 dry fruits per kg.

Nutmeg (*Myristica fragrans* Houtt.) – Myristicaceae

Type Large, evergreen tree, 10–20 m tall, to a greater or lesser extent dioecious. Both male and female plants occur but they sometimes bear flowers of the other sex in a variable percentage.

Root system Fairly close to the surface, closely interwoven.

Trunk Grey-coloured bark; smooth, grey branches; a reddish latex is present in the bark.

Leaves Alternate, single, petiolated, without stipules. Petioles 1 cm long. Elliptical, lanceolated lamina, pointed at the end, base attenuated towards the petiole, 5–15 cm long × 3–7 cm wide.

Inflorescence Axillary cymes, differing in appearance according to flower sex. Male cymes of six to 10 flowers; female cymes of two to three flowers.

Flowers Regular, unisexual, pale yellow. Perianth three-lobed. Male flower ± 20 stamens. Female flower: superior, unilocular ovary with one ovule.

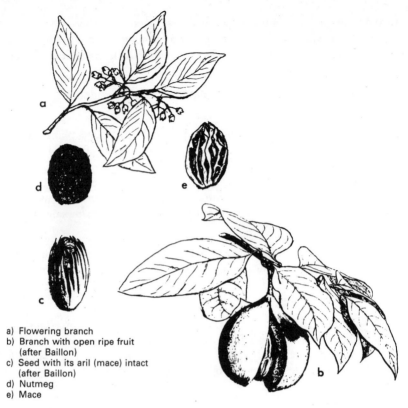

a) Flowering branch
b) Branch with open ripe fruit
   (after Baillon)
c) Seed with its aril (mace) intact
   (after Baillon)
d) Nutmeg
e) Mace

Fig 6   *Nutmeg (*Myristica fragrans *Houtt.)*

Fruit   Drupe pale yellow when ripe, fleshy, ovoid and pendant, 6–9 cm long × 5–8 cm wide, opening into two segments when mature.

Seeds   Ovoid, 3–4 cm long × 2 cm wide, covered with a lustrous, dark brown, woody testa, which is more or less completely covered with a fleshy, reddish orange, lacinated aril. This is **mace**. When the aril and the coriaceous testa have been removed, the seed is **nutmeg** which is sold commercially. 130 to 220 nutmegs = 1 kg.

Herbaceous plants with rhizomes (Zingiberaceae)

Ginger (*Zingiber officinale* Rosc.)

Type   Herbaceous perennial with rhizomes.

Root system   Rhizomes covered with scaly leaves, branching horizontally into fleshy tubers, arranged in irregular, hand-like structures (fresh, commercial ginger), pale yellow in cross-section.

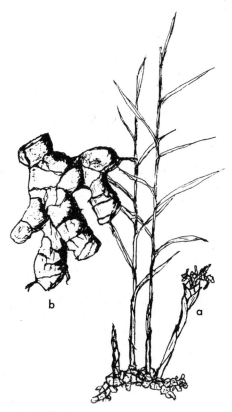

a) General view showing sterile stems,
   flower-bearing stem and rhizome
b) Fresh ginger

Fig 7 *Ginger (*Zingiber officinale *Rosc.)*

Stems Erect and vertical, generally sterile, covered with leaf sheaths, 0.60–1.50 m high.

Leaves Alternate, sessile, distichous. Linear, lanceolate, acuminate lamina 15–20 cm long × 2–3 cm wide, continuing into a transparent sheath on the stem.

Inflorescence Dense spike, 5 cm long × 2–3 cm wide, consisting of several imbricated bracts; carried at the end of a leafless stem but covered with sheath-like, tightly-packed, short scales at the base of the scape which become longer and looser as they approach the spike.

Flowers Arising in ones or twos at the axil of a bract. Greenish calyx; three sepals, joined at the base. Yellowish-orange corolla; three

21

petals, joined at the base. Three stamens, only one of which is fertile. The two sterile stamens are joined together to form a blade, 2 cm long × 1.5 cm wide, divided into three lobes. This blade (lip) is reddish purple with lighter patches. Inferior, trilocular ovary with numerous ovules. Stigmata in a fringed disc.

Fruit Capsule with three loculi; fruits are very rarely found.

Seeds Angular, small, black, arillated; very rarely develop.

Turmeric (*Curcuma domestica* Val.)

Type Herbaceous perennial with rhizomes.

Root system Rhizome, from which arise ellipsoid primary tubers, 5 cm long × 2.5 cm wide, bearing numerous, approximately cylindrical, straight or slightly curved rhizomes 5–8 cm long × 1.5 cm in diameter. These have a characteristic smell and taste.

Stems Erect, vertical, 1 m high, carrying six to 10 leaves, the sheaths of which cover the stem. The point where the petiole joins the

General view showing sterile stem,
floral spike and rhizomes

Fig 8 *Turmeric (*Curcuma domestica *Val.)*

stem is marked by a lip (ligule). At this point the sheath is covered with fine hairs.

Leaves Limp, alternate, distichous and petiolated. Lanceolated lamina 30–50 cm long × 7–8 cm wide.

Inflorescence Cylindrical spike, arising at the base of a stem, 10–15 cm long × 5–7 cm wide, formed of imbricated, dark green bracts, in the axils of which the flowers appear, one for each bract.

Flowers Short calyx. Corolla tubular at the base, then divided into three unequal, yellow lobes. Inferior, trilocular ovary; numerous ovules.

Fruit Rarely found.

Seeds Description not available.

a) Sterile stem and fertile stem with
   inflorescence and young capsules
b) Mature capsules
c) Seed
d) Transverse section of seed

Fig 9 *Cardamom (*Elettaria cardamomum *Maton var.* miniscula *Burkill)*

Cardamom (*Elettaria cardamomum* Maton var. *minuscula* Burkill)

Type   Herbaceous perennial with rhizomes.

Root system   Rhizome, orange in section, gnarled appearance with surface roots.

Stems   Sterile: 2.5–3.5 m high, covered with leaf sheaths. Fertile: often initially horizontal, later becoming erect; leaves reduced to scales.

Leaves   Alternate, sessile, forming sheaths 5–6 cm long around the stems. Linear, lanceolate lamina, 50 cm long × 4–5 cm wide.

Inflorescence   Loose spike.

Flowers   Yellow and blue; inferior, trilocular ovary, numerous ovules.

Fruits   Yellowish green to yellow, ovoid capsule, pointed at the tip and triangular in section; three loculi, 1–2 cm long × 0.5–1 cm wide. Five to seven seeds per loculus, the internal walls of which are cotton-like. Dried capsules: 6860 per kg.

Seeds   Ovoid, compressed on the sides and angular, 0.2–0.4 cm long. Grainy surface with transverse stripes along the entire length. Small, thin, colourless, membraneous aril; pale orange to cream testa turning black on drying. Characteristic aromatic odour. White kernel. 44 000 seeds per kg.

Melegueta pepper (*Aframomum melegueta* (Rosc.) K. Schum.)

Type   Herbaceous perennial with rhizomes.

Root system   Short rhizome, scaly with surface roots.

Stems   0.9 m–1.2 m high, covered by leaf sheaths up to 2 m in length.

Leaves   Alternate, sessile, continuing into a sheath on the stem, distichous. Lamina 18–22 cm long × 2 cm wide, narrowing progressively towards the base, acuminate at the tip; numerous veins; short, rounded ligule.

Inflorescence   Very short, arising at the base of a leaf-bearing stem: with one flower in two rows; sometimes two reddish bracts.

Flowers   Lilac pink, trumpet-shaped, pale mauve and large, up to 13 cm long, 4–9 cm in diameter. A single fertile stamen.

Fruit   Ovoid, then tapering to a point, surrounded by the permanent calyx. Red fruit containing white pulp surrounding 60–100 seeds.

Seeds   0.4–0.5 cm long, brown, aromatic, with a grainy testa; white kernel.

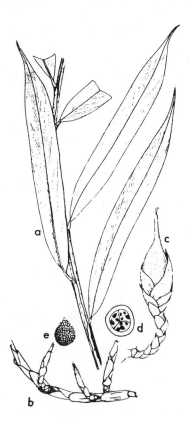

a) Stem fragment
b) Rhizome
c) Capsule
d) Transverse section of capsule
e) Seed

Fig 10   *Melegueta pepper* (Aframomum melegueta *Rosc. K. Schum.) (Reproduced with permission from Van Harten (1970)* Economie Botany, *Vol. 24, pp. 208–16)*

2.4   *Growing areas: limitations imposed by the climate and soil*

As has already been seen, the species examined here all originated in regions either with tropical rainforests or in the equatorial zone, both having a hot, humid climate. Clearly, this results in fairly rigorous climatic limitations, details of which are given below.

Rainfall and humidity

The tropical climate in the northern hemisphere is traditionally characterised by a rainy season lasting 8 to 10 months of the year, from approximately March/April to October/November. This is followed by a fairly severe dry season (less than 50 mm of rain per month) lasting two to four months from November/December to March/April. In the equatorial climate a short, fairly marked dry season divides the rainy season into two unequal periods. This occurs in July/August in the northern hemisphere.

In these two types of climate, the annual rainfall generally exceeds 1800 mm and can be as high as 4000 mm. Rainfall as heavy as this coupled with an average annual temperature of around 25°C, leads to high atmospheric humidity which, in the rainy season at least, is always 90–95% at night and rarely falls below 60% during the day.

The species studied here respond well to these rainfall and humidity patterns, with a number of specific variations regarding the length and severity of the dry season. For many of them (black pepper, cloves, nutmeg and vanilla) the dry season encourages flowering followed by fruit and seed production.

The **clove plant** illustrates this phenomenon. The vegetative growth of the clove plantations on the east coast of Madagascar, with 3300 mm of rain per annum and one to two months of a so-called dry season with up to 230 mm of rainfall, is excellent, but flowering and production are not as good as in Zanzibar, where the annual rainfall does not exceed 2000 mm with two definite dry seasons, but where the vegetative growth of cloves is not as vigorous.

Black pepper, which thrives on the west coast of India in regions where annual rainfall exceeds 3000 mm and can reach 5000 mm, can also grow adequately in equatorial climates where the annual rainfall is between 1700 and 2000 mm with fairly short dry seasons. These dry periods encourage ripening and are useful for timing harvesting.

Temperature

The average temperature should be consistently high: between 26°C and 30°C for the two 'vine' species and the four 'tree' species. The Zingiberaceae, however, thrive on lower average temperatures of around 22°C but can tolerate much higher temperatures. The average annual temperature, which is given as a guide, often hides considerable daily variations, particularly in the dry season, between the minimum night-time and maximum day-time temperatures, for example from +16°C at night to +35°C during the day.

Soil type

Certain basic soil requirements are common to all the species studied, and others, which are less general, are more specific to individual species.

A general requirement which is essential is good soil drainage without prolonged waterlogging, which eliminates marshy soils, peat bogs and generally hydromorphic soils which may nevertheless be rich in nutrients.

The pH of the soil is significant in some cases. **Allspice** prefers chalky soils with a pH of less than 7, but tolerates neutral or even slightly acid soils provided the drainage is adequate. **Black pepper** has been shown to grow well in soils with a pH of 6.5, but also in more acid or even very acid soils with a pH of 4.5–5. **Cinnamon** behaves rather differently. In the Seychelles it grows well in the acid soils of the granite-based islands of this archipelago, but grows more slowly in the neutral or alkaline soils of the islands of coral origin which are chalk-based.

The texture of the soil also affects growth and in some cases the product itself. This is true in particular with the rhizomatous Zingiberaceae (**ginger**, **turmeric**). Development of the rhizomes is inhibited in soils with a high coarse gravel content or physically impeded where soils are too heavy. In Sri Lanka, **cinnamon** grows more readily on lateritic soils rich in gravel than on fine, sandy soils. However, better quality bark is obtained from trees which grow on the latter. Waterlogged soils lead to poorer growth and lower quality bark which acquires a bitter taste and is less aromatic.

To summarise, the range of soils suitable for growing spice plants is fairly wide. Soils rich in humus are always desirable, particularly for **vanilla**; a high mineral content is favourable but not essential and will not compensate for poor drainage or inadequate rainfall.

> *The ability of spice plants to adapt to various types of soil is relatively good but varies according to species; good drainage is, however, essential for all species.*

3 Propagation and nursery management

3.1 *Types of cultivation*

There are several different types of spice-producing plantation, distinguished by the surface area under cultivation, the intensity of cultivation and the method of financing.

Small-scale domestic cultivation

The small-holding
This refers to plots cultivated around the dwelling or at a short distance from it. These plantations near the house benefit from a certain degree of attention and the application of household refuse and require minimum maintenance. Some of the species studied are sometimes grown under these conditions. In India, in the western coastal area to the south of Trivandrum, pure cultivation of **black pepper** is carried out on living supports. Another example is the cultivation of **cloves** on the island of Zanzibar, where many of the 'plantations' have fewer than fifty trees. Ginger and turmeric are also frequently grown in small garden plots.

   These small-holdings also have the characteristic of being tended solely by the family.

Open field cultivation
These plantations vary enormously with regard to the technology used and the intensity of cultivation. A mature plantation of **nutmeg, allspice** and **clove** trees requires little maintenance, the most labour-intensive period of the year being the harvest. The same roughly applies to **cinnamon**, except for the fact that formative pruning in the early years of growth is very labour-intensive and processing the harvested crop requires care and a great deal of skill.

   Open field cultivation of vines (**black pepper, vanilla**) and various members of the family Zingiberaceae forms the highest percentage of spices grown, with commercial spice plantations not having the same importance as, for example, in coffee, rubber or oil palm cultivation.

This type of plantation employs mainly family labour but occasionally additional outside paid labour is used, particularly during the harvesting of cloves in Madagascar and Zanzibar, or for certain growing techniques such as fertilising vanilla in Madagascar.

Commercial plantations

This category encompasses plantations run by individuals, companies or official bodies which have the considerable capital needed to plant the crops, build the premises required for processing the harvested crop, housing the agricultural equipment and housing the workforce. As previously stated, there are only a few of these large private or state plantations in existence. **Black pepper** plantations can be found in Nossi-Bé (Malagasy Republic), **nutmeg** plantations in Grenada and **ginger** plantations in Australia.

Commercial plantations generally cover a fairly wide area, use modern growing methods, process the final product which is almost always entirely exported, and apply the results of agricultural research, when this exists.

In the past few decades, the agricultural advisory services have also strived to enable small-holders to benefit from the results published by Research Institutes and Departments, thus improving the general level of production both in terms of quantity and quality. Examples of this can be seen in Grenada.

3.2 *Factors affecting the choice of growing area*

This section deals with the cultivation of spice plants in areas where they are not indigenous. This does, of course, presuppose that the potential growers have reliable information on the characteristics of the regions under consideration.

Climate

In tropical regions, reliable rainfall records which go back a long way are rare, except in the main agricultural centres. It is essential to have reliable information on the rainfall distribution pattern, including the time of year when the dry season(s) occur, their duration and their severity. It should be noted that all the spices studied (except for ginger) require a minimum rainfall of 1800–2000 mm/year, and that a well-defined but short dry season is beneficial for fruiting. This applies to black pepper and vanilla in particular.

There is little value in knowing the average temperatures. Minimum and maximum temperatures, however, are of particular importance if high-altitude sites are chosen. Under such conditions the extremes are more marked and, except for ginger, which is more tolerant of such conditions, excessively low minimum temperatures are to be avoided.

A final climatic characteristic which is only measured in large metereological centres, is wind pattern. Any risk of cyclones must be taken into consideration and, if possible, the plantation should be sited where this phenomenon is unlikely to occur. The 'wind' factor is particularly important where **clove trees** are grown, as the wood of these trees breaks easily. Consequently, they should be planted in zones unlikely to be subjected to violent winds. **Nutmeg** is also susceptible to wind, but to a lesser extent.

Soils

Good drainage is essential; this excludes hydromorphic soils, even if their high mineral content appears attractive. The ideal pH is generally slightly acid, except for **allspice**, which prefers neutral or slightly alkaline soils. Special consideration must be given to the texture of the soil for **ginger** and **turmeric**, which both prefer a soil free of stones or coarse gravel so that their underground root systems can develop without being impeded.

Topography and siting of the plantation

Flat sites are preferable in theory, but if circumstances make it necessary to plant on slopes, arrangements must be made to protect and to preserve the soil by terracing if the gradient exceeds 3 per cent. This is particularly important for **ginger** and **turmeric**, where soil preparation for a high density crop involves the whole plantation and where the cultivation of large areas makes the soil more sensitive to the impact of rain and run-off.

Proximity to the sea should be avoided as saline soils are not suitable for most spice crops. It was once thought that sea spray was necessary for cloves to flourish. This is not now accepted and, if this species does not grow well away from the coast and at higher altitudes, its poor growth will be due to an unfavourable change in the climate.

3.3 *Cultivation systems*

Among the spices studied in this volume, black pepper, vanilla, cinnamon, cloves, allspice and nutmeg are all perennials which will be productive for many years. Although the life of a pepper or vanilla plantation is only about 15 years, the four other perennial species can survive for as long as 50 to 100 years! The cultivation systems used for these species are therefore very different from those of the Zingiberaceae, which have a much shorter growing cycle of one or two years, although they are also perennials. In tropical agriculture, growing two or more species together is a very widespread practice, particularly for food crops. This form of intercropping is also used for the species examined here, but to a lesser extent. It is therefore necessary to distinguish between a pure and a mixed crop.

Pure crops

This is the most common planting system used for intensive cultivation in commercial plantations, and is used for rubber, cocoa and oil palm. The space between the rows of trees, known as the **interrow**, can be treated in various ways. It can be kept 'clean' by repeated weeding or mulching or even, as is most frequently the case, covered with self-sown vegetation which becomes less dense as the plantation matures and the branches meet and restrict the penetration of sunlight.

In the intensive cultivation of **black pepper** in Sarawak, the soil is kept clean. However, it is generally sufficient to cut back the natural vegetation as in the cultivation of **cloves**, **vanilla** and **nutmeg**.

Cover plants such as those used in coffee, rubber and oil palm plantations, are rarely used in spice cultivation outside research stations. If sown at all, they tend to be commonly used legumes such as, *Mimosa invisa* var. *inermis* used in black pepper crops grown in the Central African Republic. In Madagascar *Vigna hosei* is favoured, together with *Centrosema pubescens* and *Pueraria phaseoloides* in **clove** plantations. *Centrosema pubescens* is also recommended in **clove** plantations in Indonesia.

Mixed cropping

Some crops are virtually never interplanted with others. This is true for **cinnamon**, **allspice** and **cardamom** which are almost always grown as a pure crop, as is **vanilla**, except on Réunion as will be described later. The other species of spice plants, however, are commonly intercropped with other food plants.

Black pepper

In India, in the Madras area, black pepper is established in tea, coffee and mandarin plantations; the shade trees of the main crop serving as living supports for the pepper vines.

In Sri Lanka, black pepper, cloves and even nutmeg are all grown under coconut palms. In India also, mixed cultivation is practised with the areca palm serving as a living support; with irrigation being applied

Fig 11   *Pepper plants on living supports (areca palms). Kampuchea (IRAT photographic library)*

to the spice crops. Trials have shown that the yield in nuts of the areca palm is totally unaffected by the presence of the pepper vine (Fig 11).

Vanilla

On Réunion, vanilla has been intercropped for some time with sugar cane, using a range of methods according to the ratio of rows of vanilla plants to rows of sugar cane. Experience has shown that two rows of sugar cane plus two rows of vanilla plants, or four rows of sugar cane plus two rows of vanilla, are effective combinations from the point of view of the yield and harvesting and transportation requirements of the sugar cane. The vanilla plants can also be planted in rows on 0.4 m high ridges, spaced 3.4 m apart and separated by an intermediary row of sugar cane. In the row, the vanilla vines climbing up the living supports are 1.2 m apart. The advantages of this mixed intensive cultivation system are that it provides shading and acts as a windbreak, with organic matter being supplied by the sugar cane which also grows vigorously. Where the crop arrangement consists of one row of vanilla plants and one row of sugar cane with a large space between them, legumes may be grown in the space between the vanilla plants and/or between the vanilla plants and the sugar cane during the first and even the second year. With whatever system used, it is essential to avoid weeding or scraping the earth from around the base of the vanilla plants, since they have a fragile surface root system.

Cloves
In Zanzibar, cloves are often planted under coconut palms, together with bananas or manioc. In Madagascar, a successful combination is considered to be cloves with cocoa or robusta coffee, but not with manioc.

Ginger
In Sri Lanka and on the islands of Fiji, ginger is often grown under coconut palms. In South Africa, on intensively cultivated plantations, trials with maize, planted in every fourth interrow, and with haricot beans, planted in every interrow, showed that the yield and quality of the ginger was reduced. Additionally, ginger is often interplanted with turmeric.

Turmeric
This crop is also found growing under coconut palms in Sri Lanka, India and on the Fiji islands. Trials carried out in India gave the following yields: 4.8 tonnes/hectare in association with coconut palms, 7 tonnes/hectare as a sole crop.

Planting turmeric with banana palms in India (Gujarat) is considered to be a satisfactory combination, but intercropping with maize in eastern Bengal has been less successful. More complex combinations have been found in garden plantations. The crop normally grows over a period of two years. In the first year, turmeric, fenugreek and haricot beans can be grown and for part of the second year, a combination of onions, beetroot and ginger has been found to be successful.

In traditional agriculture there are numerous examples of spice plants growing together with one or more other crops. In most cases the yield from these combined crops is better overall than that of a sole crop.

---

4 Vegetative propagation, genetic improvement and selection

Given the considerable differences which exist between the three groups of spice plants examined in this book, it is difficult to comment on characteristics which are common to the selection and improvement work carried out on these plants, except that, for various reasons, they have not given very significant results so far. The various groups have therefore been given separate treatment in this chapter.

4.1 Vines

Black pepper

A large number of varieties of *Piper nigrum* can be found in the wild state due to propagation from fruits eaten by birds, the seeds of which germinate in the droppings. For centuries, man has selected outstanding and high-yielding plants which, when multiplied through cuttings, retained their original characteristics. For example, the flower of the **black pepper** plant is very complex. Some types have a high percentage of bisexual flowers. The latter, which are naturally more productive, have been favourably selected. In addition, a fairly high number of different clones are cultivated in countries where the pepper plant is grown, namely, India, Indonesia and Kampuchea. From among these, two main characteristics stand out:
- selections with large leaves and long internodes;
- selections with small leaves and shorter internodes.

These differences in leaf morphology are accompanied by differences in the shapes of the berries, and also physiological differences. To elucidate on this, the following is a comparison of a number of characteristics from two classical Indonesian varieties: **Lampong**, which has large leaves, and **Bangka**, which has small leaves (after Maistre).

The 'Lampong' type, in India, includes the 'Balamkotta' variety and, in Kampuchea, the 'Phnom-Pon' variety. The 'Bangka' type in Kampuchea includes the 'Kamchay' variety. The Indonesian variety 'Belantoeng' was

Table 7 *Comparison of two Indonesian varieties*

Lampong (Kawur)	Bangka (Muntok)
Thick but fragile stem	Coriaceous stem
Ample horizontal branches	Short pendant branches
First flowering at two years	Early flowering
Large bunches of regularly abundant fruits	Small short spikes
Small peppercorns, light in colour and irregular in size	Large peppercorns, off-white in colour and irregular in size
Berries mature in 9 months; harvesting is earlier than with Bangka	Berries mature in 10 months; harvesting is later than with Lampong
Short harvesting period (5 to 6 rounds)	Longer harvesting period (more than 6 rounds)
Young vines grow fairly well in poor soils	Young vines grow weakly in poor soils
Longevity: no more than 20 years	Longevity: more than 30 years

introduced into Madagascar more than fifty years ago and more recently into the Central African republic in 1954. This is a variety of the 'Lampong' type which is relatively resistant to collar rot (see section 6.1). Selecting clones resistant to this disease, which ravages plantations in Brazil in particular, is now one of the main aims of the selectors.

Some clones which produce a good yield and have good resistance to collar disease, IV–1 and IV–38 in particular, have been identified in Madagascar at the Ivoloina research station. The problem with black pepper and vanilla plants, which we shall examine next, is the gradual reduction in the level of tolerance to collar disease, a problem which is common to all perennial spice crops and the source of a great deal of disappointment.

Vanilla

Like the pepper plant, vanilla is also vulnerable to a serious disease of the roots and collar which does not respond to fungicides. The only solution, therefore, appeared to be to obtain clones which are resistant to the disease. Work was carried out on this problem up to 1973, mainly at the IRAT Research Station at Antalaha, in the North East of the Republic of Madagascar. The main objective was to create hybrids between *Vanilla fragrans* and other species of *Vanilla* which appeared to have improved resistance to the disease, but which had pods without the aromatic qualities of *V. fragrans*. Three species were used: *V. tahitensis*, *V. phoeantha* and *V. pompona*.

Although hybridisation is not difficult to carry out, seed germination problems make it necessary to develop very elaborate laboratory techniques. It is also known that the seed cannot germinate unless a microscopic fungus (*Rhizoctonia* sp.) is present to initiate the development of the embryo by penetrating the seed. In addition, the young plants can only be raised in the laboratory.

From the time when the seed is removed from the pod to the stage where the resulting plants can be planted out in the field, three years will have passed. The vine will not flower before it is three years old, and often far later. These figures demonstrate the inevitable slowness of any work directed towards genetic improvement in the vanilla plant.

As no resistance test which involved artificially inoculating the disease was found to be of any obvious value, the workers assessing resistance had to be satisfied simply with monitoring the behaviour of the various hybrids in the field. This work, which unfortunately was discontinued in 1974 for non-scientific reasons, did not produce any convincing results. The hybrids *V. fragrans* x *V. tahitensis* (var. Haapape) grew rapidly, had good and often exceptional fertility but were scarcely any more resistant to collar disease than their parents.

This research could be resumed if vanilla cultivation was given greater priority. However, over the past decade this has not been the case, mainly due to the stagnation in production and demand.

4.2 Trees

In addition to the difficulties outlined with the two vine species already described, there is the major problem of the time it takes to improve trees which do not come into production before ten or fifteen years from planting, such as **cloves**, **allspice** and **nutmeg**. For **cinnamon**, which comes into production a little sooner at six years, the nature of the product (the bark) makes evaluation difficult, if it is only based on weight, as quality criteria are very important. There does not appear to be any current genetic improvement work being carried out on varieties of **cinnamon** and **allspice**.

Selection work has been initiated on **cloves**, using populations obtained from seeds harvested from plantations where unwanted trees (those with little resistance to disease and low yields) had been removed. In Java, attempts are also being made to identify the best adult trees in selected plantations and to multiply these using cuttings.

Approximately the same procedure is being followed for **nutmeg**, which has a great range of individual tree types. Significant differences can be seen in various plantations between the morphology of the leaves, flowers and fruits, and also production. It has already been stated that the nutmeg tree is quite distinctly dioecious; the 'male' plants bearing a small number of fruits, while the 'female' plants have more or less completely female characteristics, producing most of the total.

It is clear that during the selection work the plants with the most 'female' characteristics should be retained. These trees are propagated by vegetative means such as grafting or layering. This is the selection procedure followed in Grenada.

4.3 Herbaceous, rhizomatous plants (Zingiberaceae)

As **ginger** and **turmeric** virtually never produce fruits and seeds, the selector has to work on material which has been multiplied vegetatively for a long time and in which few clones can be distinguished. The main differences are to be found in the colour of the rhizome, which may be white, yellowish-white or blue, and in the quantity of fibres present in the rhizome. Listed below are some of the most widely used clones:

- India: 'Burdwan', 'Maran', 'Narasapattam', 'Karakkal'
- Brazil: 'Rio de Janeiro'
- China: 'China'

These clones are tested for several characteristics, such as productivity, disease-resistance, essential oil content, oleoresin content and fibre content. In India, the 'Burdwan' and 'Rio de Janeiro' varieties do well in all these tests.

Work is being carried out in India at the University of Kerala where, owing to treatment with colchicine, it has been possible to obtain tetraploid plants which are more vigorous in all respects than the original diploids and from which new plants are being selected.

Turmeric selection is very similar to **ginger** selection. In India the clones 'Armoor', 'Erode', 'Salem' and 'Mannuthy' are used and, more recently, 'Krishna', which appears to be more productive than the others.

Finally, selection work on **cardamom** is at a fairly advanced stage. As with ginger and turmeric, clones are being tested in India at the Mudigere Research Station. The most widespread variety, 'Malabar', is looking very promising in these trials. The capsules of this variety vary greatly in size and shape but, in general, are not deeply furrowed and are approximately ovoid, whereas those of the 'Mysore' variety are larger, deeply furrowed, triangular in section and yellow when mature.

5 Cultural techniques

5.1 *Soil and site preparation*

Vines

Preparing the soil for prospective pepper or vanilla plantations must take into account the need to supply each vine with a support or stake upon which it can climb. Later (see 5.3 page 48), it will be seen that these supports are divided into two categories: non-living and living. In the former, site preparation is unaffected because it is possible to put the non-living support, for example a wooden stake, in place at any time after the soil has been cultivated by general ploughing or hole-pre-paration. Where living supports are used, these must be established before taking the cuttings from the pepper or vanilla plants. The supports most often used for pepper are either plants which are already in the plantation (rubber, for example) or trees from original forest growth, left in place during land clearance. In the latter case, the fact that the supports are already present makes it essential that the holes at the foot of each support are made by hand.

In intensive pepper-growing regions such as Kampuchea, cleared, wooded areas are used. The forest is felled and the stumps removed; unusable, smaller pieces of wood being burnt on site and the ashes spread on the soil. The ground is then hoed to a depth of about 30 cm and formed into long ridges perpendicular to the slope. If the ground only slopes gently (less than 3 per cent), ridging is not necessary as there is little risk of erosion by run-off. The holes evacuated are approximately 0.4 m in diameter and 0.4 m deep and, insofar as is possible, are filled with 'good soil'. This 'good soil' is ideally enriched with organic fertiliser and forest earth.

The treatment ranges from this very careful soil preparation to a simple hole made at the foot of the support and filled with the soil which had been dug out during hole-making. This approach is the one most frequently adopted in vanilla plantations, with humus-rich earth being applied as a mulch after the cuttings have been planted out.

Trees

Here too, the hole-making technique is used after careful land clearance. The dimensions of the holes vary according to the species and, to some extent also, according to the country. For example: in Sri Lanka, **cinnamon** is planted in holes 0.3 m in diameter × 0.3 m deep; in Madagascar, **cloves** are planted in holes 0.6 m in diameter × 0.6 m deep and in Indonesia, **nutmeg** is planted in trenches 1.2 m wide × 0.9 m deep. It is advisable to make the holes at least two weeks before planting out.

Herbaceous plants with rhizomes (Zingiberaceae)

It is necessary here to draw a distinction between species of the Zingiberaceae family grown for their rhizomes, such as **ginger** and **turmeric**, and those grown for their seeds, such as **cardamom** and **Melegueta pepper**.

With ginger and turmeric, careful preparation is necessary to loosen the soil and to enable the rhizomes to develop without being hindered by physical obstacles. The soil should therefore be broken down finely before planting. In India (Malabar coast) the soil is ploughed five to six times before preparing the beds into which the **ginger** rhizomes will be planted. In Mysore state, after the soil has been ploughed four to six times to ensure that it has been broken up sufficiently, it is formed into ridges approximately 1.20 m apart and 0.15 m high. A network of small trenches or furrows may be constructed to enable excess water to run away. This is common practice in large plantations. In small garden plantations, the classical beds such as those used for vegetables are considered suitable (Jamaica). In areas where crops are irrigated by gravity, for example Bengal, the earth may be ploughed up to 12 times before planting, each ploughing being carried out after it has rained. Manure is ploughed in during one of these ploughings and, after levelling the surface, a network of irrigation trenches is excavated.

Ground preparation for **cardamom** is different as partially cleared forested land is used so as to retain a certain degree of shading. After clearing away the vegetable debris, approximately the same procedure as that described for pepper and vanilla plants is followed. Planting holes 30 cm × 45 cm × 45 cm are excavated. These holes are filled with surface soil which is usually rich in organic matter.

5.2 Propagation and planting

Vines

Black pepper and **vanilla** are now propagated solely by vegetative means, i.e. by taking cuttings. It is possible to propagate pepper by sowing seed, but it is a technique which is of little value to the planter and should be left to the research stations. This is particularly applicable to the vanilla plant. For both species, seedling multiplication is essential for work on genetic improvement but should be reserved for this type of work.

Propagation by cuttings may be either direct, i.e. carried out at the final planting site, or cuttings may be raised in a nursery or cutting laboratory.

Direct propagation by cuttings

This method is frequently used for black pepper. In pepper plantations in the Indochina Peninsula, sections of orthotropic stems approximately 50–60 cm long with five to seven nodes are used. The terminal shoot is removed, if necessary, together with any lateral branches; the leaves on the upper two nodes being retained. In Malaysia, the cutting is 'prepared' while it is still attached to the parent plant and is not removed until at least one week later, which allows the scars from the cut sections at the nodes to heal more quickly; a new terminal bud will also begin to develop. In India, sections of the stolons are often used. These are frequently very long and arise from the base of the pepper plants often taking root spontaneously at the nodes. This type of cutting is not recommended as it gives less vigorous plants which fruit later.

Cuttings taken from the vanilla plants, which are 1.50 m to 2 m in length, are longer than those used with pepper plants. They are better taken in the dry season and experience has shown (in Réunion) that a sharp blade of the grafting knife type should be used for cutting and trimming, in favour of secateurs.

The leaves of the fourth to fifth nodes from the tip are removed and the cutting is kept loosely rolled up in a cool, shaded place for two to three weeks. When ready for insertion, the cutting must be handled very carefully. The lower three to four internodes are placed in a shallow trench 3–4 cm deep and about 10 cm wide. The evacuated soil is used to loosely fill this trench. This operation is usually carried out at the beginning of the rainy season.

Preparing cuttings in a nursery

This method, which is mainly used for **pepper plants** but which can also be used for other species, enables savings to be made on planting material and has a markedly higher success rate when the cutting is finally planted out. It is the method selected when planting material is only available in small quantities and when it is important that the maximum number of cuttings should 'take'.

Fig 12 *Pepper cuttings trough at the Boukoko Research Centre. Central African Republic (Larcher)*

Fig 13 *Removing rooted pepper cuttings from the propagating trough at the Boukoko Research Centre. Central African Republic (Larcher)*

The general principle is to use short cuttings of three, two or even single internodes, treated with a growth hormone and rooted in a suitable medium. This medium is contained in cement troughs with transparent covers which can be opened to various degrees. The whole closely resembles the frames traditionally used by market gardeners, but with a much greater depth of medium. The medium is kept suitably moist by spraying once or twice a day, or more if necessary, and opening and closing the covers as necessary (Figs 12 and 13).

In Cameroon, at the N'Kolbisson Centre, cuttings with two nodes are used with well decomposed wood shavings as the medium. In the Central African Republic at the Boukoko Centre which, in the 1970s, supplied 150 000 to 200 000 rooted plants per annum, the medium was also based on well decomposed wood shavings and coarse sawdust but cuttings with three nodes were used.

An example of more intensive methods used in propagation by cuttings is given by the specialist centre of Babia in New Guinea, where the cuttings consist of a single internode and are therefore very short, about 6–7 cm. The rooting medium consists of a 45 cm deep layer of vermiculite. Air humidity is maintained by mist spraying under pressure at a rate of 2.5 l/hr.

Whatever the method used, when the cutting has rooted, which may take from four to eight weeks, it is transferred to a locally made container, or preferably a black polythene bag containing a mixture of 'good forest earth', compost and even manure if this is available. At the Babia Centre, for example, these bags are normally filled with a mixture consisting of:

⅛ alluvial soil,
⅛ peat,
⅛ sand and
⅜ leaf mould.

The plants are kept under light shade and sprayed regularly until they are ready to be transported to their final places in the plot.

Advanced multiplication techniques: tissue cultures

Tissue culture which allows for the rapid multiplication of varieties which are of interest because of various factors such as yield, state of health (no viruses for example) or resistance to disease, has become part of horticultural practice for many species such as orchids.

For the most important spice plants, work is still only at a preliminary stage, but work is currently being carried out on this technique for **black pepper** in Malaysia, **vanilla** in Réunion, **ginger** in India and South Africa, **turmeric** in India and **cardamom** in India. These *in-vitro* cultivation techniques are clearly based in the laboratory, but they already have a role to play as a supplement to the genetic improvement work being carried out, as has already been seen in Chapter 4.

Trees

Direct sowing and propagation by cuttings

Sowing at a specific spacing in the plantation is only practised very rarely for the four spice species studied in this text. In Sri Lanka, **cinnamon** is sometimes propagated using fragments of rooted stump, planted at a definite spacing. As each tree has several stems, up to about ten in number, these stems are cut back to approximately 15 cm from the ground and the stump is then divided into as many pieces as there are stems.

Self-sown plants should also be included here. These may originate from fruit eaten by birds (**cinnamon** and **allspice**) or may simply be seeds which have fallen to the foot of the tree (**nutmeg** and **cloves**) and which have germinated successfully. In the Seychelles, there is a species of martin which is responsible for the development of small forests of cinnamon trees on these islands.

Seedlings raised in a nursery
This is clearly the most reliable method. The techniques used and the time the seedlings spend in the nursery vary according to the species. The fruits used for **cinnamon** propagation in Sri Lanka are well-formed, and either in the process of ripening or, preferably, fully ripe. This is often difficult to achieve as ripe fruits are very much sought after by birds. The seeds are extracted by rubbing the fruits together, removing the pulp, washing the seeds in water and drying them in the shade. The seeds are sown in groups of eight, spaced at 15 cm × 20 cm at a depth of 2 cm. Germination occurs after two to three weeks. When the plants are about 15 cm high, the shading is removed and pricking out takes place to leave a larger space between the plants of 30 cm × 30 cm or 40 cm × 40 cm. The plants remain in this second nursery for four to five months with light shading or no shading at all until final planting out. The calendar of tasks is therefore as follows:
- July–August: sowing
- December: picking out
- April–May: planting out

Clove plants in Madagascar require slightly less work. Since they are known to be intolerant of root disturbance, as in pricking out, the seeds of this species are sown immediately after harvesting at a spacing of 30 cm × 30 cm. The seeds germinate in five weeks. The plants spend nine to twelve months in the nursery before final planting out.

A more reliable but slightly more labour-intensive method is to replace the nursery bed with containers filled with earth. This enables the plants to be planted with their root balls intact. These containers may be baskets woven from locally grown bamboo-type canes, or polythene bags which are now generally used in coffee plantations or forestry nurseries. Two or three seeds are planted in each container and after germination, the most vigorous of the plants which has developed will be retained.

Nutmeg, like **allspice** is dioecious. It is in the interest of the planter to retain in his plantation, only the minimum number of male plants necessary for fertilisation and to have the maximum number of female fruit-producing plants. Unfortunately, as the nutmeg plant will be between four and eight years old before its first flowering, it is not possible to select the female plants in the nursery.

Nutmeg seeds must be sown within 24 hours of harvesting, as the germination potential is very short-lived. The seeds are sown to a depth of 6 cm at a spacing 40 cm × 40 cm. They germinate within four to five weeks and the plants normally remain in the nursery up to the age of six months. They will then be 15 to 20 cm high and can be transferred to their permanent site.

Grafting

Grafting is rarely used for **black pepper** and **vanilla**, except for research puposes in experimental stations. It is used fairly commonly, however, for **nutmeg** in Grenada and very commonly for **allspice** in Jamaica. These two species are dioecious and it is advantageous if plants of which the sex is definitely known can be planted out. A useful grafting method involves the sex of the scion graft being preserved whatever the sex of the stock plant. For allspice plants aged 18 to 24 months, the approach grafting method is used. The young scion plant and the branch of the stock plant which is to receive the graft are placed into close contact after a slice of stem, about 6 cm long, has been removed from each. The graft is kept in position by a special type of plastic band. Watering is carried out regularly and the graft, if it is to be successful, will 'take' within three months. After being separated from the stock plant, the grafted young plant is then 'hardened off' in the nursery for three to four months before being planted out. This method is 95 per cent successful for **allspice** but much less so for **nutmeg**, for which layering is more suitable.

Layering

This propagation technique is sometimes used in India for **black pepper**, using the stems (stolons) which grow on the soil surface and which often root spontaneously. This method is not often used for pepper however, as it is slow and difficult to apply to intensive propagation systems, having a success rate of less than 50 per cent. It is, however, widely used for **nutmeg** in Grenada. In **air layering**, branches approximately 1 cm in diameter are used. A slit approximately 5 cm long is cut into the stems and the two edges of this slit are kept apart by introducing a small piece of bamboo. The exposed tissues of the slit are lightly dusted with a rooting powder before being wrapped in a sleeve of moss, peat or coir, extending beyond the area by 10 cm below and 5 cm above. The sleeve is wrapped in a transparent polythene sheet which holds the rooting medium firmly in place and prevents water loss. The sleeve is kept damp by occasionally opening the top and moistening the contents. Rooting occurs from four months to one year later. When root-development is visible, the layers are removed from the parent branch and transferred to special troughs where they are initially watered three times a day. They are gradually hardened off before being planted in their final positions. The hardening may take six to eight weeks from the separation of the rooted layers. In all, there is a 30 to 40 per cent success rate.

Zingiberaceae: propagation by rhizomes

For **ginger** and **turmeric** species, the seeds of which are virtually unknown, propagation is normally carried out using a small portion of rhizome. For the other two species, **cardamom** and **melegueta pepper**, it is normal to use either seeds or rhizome portions.

Rhizome portions used as propagating material must each have at least one dormant bud or **eye**. These are planted in shallow holes at a depth of 5 cm. Depending on the spacing used, the quantity of planting material required ranges from 900 to 1400 kg/hectare. This method, which is used in the State of Kerala, undoubtedly consumes more planting material than is used in most of the other Indian States. In other States, the weight of seeds is less, for example, 700 kg/hectare in the Punjab and 350 kg in western Bengal. Over a considerable period, agricultural trials have shown that the larger the initial portions of rhizome used, the higher the yield obtained. In normal agricultural practice, organic and mineral fertiliser application, mulching, weed, pest and disease control techniques are used.

In Australia, namely Queensland, where planting is carried out by machine, using a potato planter at a rate of 1000 m²/hour, the rhizome portions used each weigh 70 to 80 g. Under these conditions, 4 to 6 tonnes per hectare of rhizome pieces are used and it is thought that a planting level of up to 10 tonnes/hectare is economically viable.

The rhizome portions are obtained from special fields used for producing propagating material. The soils of these areas are nematode-free since they will have been treated with special chemicals such as nematicides. The rhizomes are harvested six weeks before they are required and are treated with Benlate, a fungicide, immediately before planting.

Cardamom, which up to the 1950s was normally propagated in the same way as **ginger** and **turmeric**, is now propagated by seeds, particularly in regions which are severely affected by mosaic virus. This virus, which spreads rapidly when propagation is carried out vegetatively, is not present in the seeds. Unfortunately, plants grown from seed produce their first harvest after five years compared with only three years for those which have developed from rhizomes. Propagation by seed involves the use of nurseries and sowing the seeds as soon as possible after harvest.

The germination rate drops rapidly, from 75 per cent at the time of harvesting, to 46 per cent two weeks later and to only 6 per cent, 105 days after harvesting. Soaking the seeds for ten minutes in a 25 per cent solution of nitric acid (HNO_3) considerably improves germination.

After being carefully washed, the seeds are sown in shallow drills 3–4 cm apart, with the same distance between the seeds and are covered with chopped, well rotted mulch. Germination begins one month after sowing and is staggered over several months. At one year old, the plants are transferred to a second nursery where they remain for a further year before being planted out.

With **melegueta pepper**, which is cultivated without much attention to detail in several African countries, particularly in Ghana, sowing is either by broadcasting on roughly hoed land or slightly more care is taken in sowing seeds in prepared planting holes around which the soil surface has been cleaned and hoed.

General guidelines for nursery management

The following is a brief review of the general principles of nursery management for each species which have not previously been described.

The soil in the nursery must be light and well-drained but it must be capable of retaining sufficient moisture after watering. The addition of a soil rich in organic matter and humus can improve a poor soil. After sowing the seed, it is sound practise to spread a layer of straw, chopped grass, crushed leaves or decomposed bagasse over the soil surface. This layer, which should be 2–3 cm thick, is very effective in conserving moisture and keeping the soil cool. Shading is indispensable for protecting the young plants from direct exposure to sunlight and can usually be provided by palm leaves or any similar available material. Shading also has the advantage of reducing the impact of heavy rainstorms and, together with a mulch, of reducing any risks associated with run-off and bed damage. The soil in the nursery must be kept free of weeds and, during watering, the beds should be regularly checked and casual weeds removed as soon as they appear. Fertiliser application to young nursery seedlings can be useful in promoting their growth before they are transplanted. Nursery workers should apply fungicidal or insecticidal treatments regularly since, given the relatively small area to be treated, this is a profitable exercise. If the plants have to be treated in the final plantation, the costs will be much greater.

Plantation tree spacing

Table 8 gives information on the plant spacings used in the open-field plantations and, unless otherwise stated, refers to pure stand cropping.

> For crops intended to be in situ for many years, the propagation nursery is a
> very important stage in their growth and development. It lasts for a relatively
> short period and covers a small area which requires tending with the greatest
> care.

Table 8 *The most commonly used spacings in spice plant cultivation (pure crops)*

Species	Spacings
Black pepper	2 m × 2 m (Kampuchea); 2.4 m × 2.4 m (Sarawak); 2.4 m to 3.6 m × 2.4 m to 3.6 m (Mysore); 2.5 m × 2.5 m (Brazil) The density of planting is always greater when non-living, rather than living supports are used
Vanilla	1.5 m × 2.5 m × 3 m; 1.2 m × 3.7 m (planted between sugar cane in Réunion)
Cinnamon	1.75 m × 2.5 m × 1.75 m to 2.5 m (Sri Lanka)
Cloves	4 m to 5 m × 4 m to 5 m (Madagascar); 6 m to 9 m × 6 m to 9 m (Zanzibar); 7 m × 8 m (IRAT recommended); 3 m to 5 m × 6 m to 7.5 (for clove leaf plantations)
Nutmeg	8 m to 9 m × 8 m to 9 m (Indonesia); 6 m to 7.5 m × 6 m to 7.5 m (Grenada)
Allspice	5.5 m × 5.5 m In hedges 2 m apart for leaf plantations
Ginger	0.25 m × 0.25 m (India – Mizoram); 0.3 m × 0.3 m (Kerala); 0.3 m × 0.8 m (Bengal); 0.3 m × 1.2 m (Mysore); 0.1 m to 0.3 m × 0.6 m (Fiji); 0.35 m × 0.5 m (Jamaica)
Turmeric	0.225 m × 0.225 m (India); 0.15 m to 0.3 m × 0.15 m to 0.3 m (Sri Lanka)
Cardamom	2 m to 2.5 m × 2 m to 2.5 m (India); 1.5 m × 1.8 m, 1.8 m to 2.1 m (Mysore variety); 2.1 m × 2.4 m (Malabar variety) in Réunion
Melegueta pepper	Spacings vary enormously as this species is almost always grown in association with others

5.3 Crop maintenance

Weeds

Weeds are unwanted in any crop as they compete with the species grown for water and soil minerals and, if they grow very large, they can also reduce the level of sunlight reaching the leaves of the species under cultivation. All these factors combine to reduce growth, particularly in young plants which are more vulnerable. In a mature plantation, as the trees grow closer together, the branches limit weed growth. Since it takes many years to reach this stage the problem must be combatted as vigorously as possible in the early stages of the growth, although this recommendation is not always followed.

Weed species

No attempt will be made here to describe in detail the weed species which may occur, as different species are found in the various countries under consideration. It is sufficient for practical reasons to distinguish between two categories of plant:

- narrow-leaved weeds, generally monocotyledons, and mainly plants of the Gramineae and Cyperaceae families;
- broad-leaved weeds, generally dicotyledons which may belong to numerous families, among which are the Compositae, Amaranthaceae, Polygonaceae, Solanaceae and Convolvulaceae.

In the former category, two pantropical species of the family Gramineae, which may become aggressive weeds, deserve mention:

- *Imperata cylindrica* ('Imperata', 'tranh' in Vietnam; 'lalang' in Malaysia): very vigorous grasses with underground rhizomes which regenerate from small portions. For this reason, it is very difficult to eliminate this species completely;
- *Paspalum conjugatum*: a very vigorous grass, together with other species in the same genus.

Mechanical weeding

This consists of uprooting the weeds with a hoe, or any other suitable tool, either throughout the entire plantation or over a limited area around each plant. This 'ring weeding' is generally carried out over an area of approximately 0.75 m to 1.5 m in radius using the base of each plant as a centre. An alternative is 'strip weeding', which involves cleaning a strip approximately 0.75 m to 1 m wide on either side of the tree row which therefore forms the median axis of this strip of clean land. Rough slashing or scything the remainder of the vegetation in the interrow completes this type of maintenance, which is exactly the same when spontaneous vegetation has been replaced by the establishment of a cover crop. Where mixed crops are grown, with irregular spacing, careful ring weeding is the rule. Clean weeding, which completely denudes the soil between the plants, is not very popular as it is difficult to carry out and leaves the soil exposed to superficial erosion by run-off during heavy rain, particularly on sloping ground.

In many situations weed control is inadequate. Where tree species are grown, two or even only one weeding round is frequently considered to be sufficient! This weeding round often takes place shortly before harvesting in order to facilitate the movement of the workers. In mature plantations where there is little vegetation in the interrows, it is feasible to have only one weeding; in young plantations however, the growth of the plant is impeded by weed competition and future production is likely to suffer. This is particularly true of the species of Zingiberaceae with rhizomes, but the producer of these crops is likely to appreciate this factor more clearly and generally carries out suitable maintenance. With the weeding of Zingiberaceae, it is imperative that hoeing only scratches the surface, with vanilla, which has a very delicate root system, it should not be carried out at all.

Chemical weeding

Herbicides are not used in spice cultivation to any great extent. Their use is known, but apart from being occasionally used on **ginger** in Australia, it has scarcely passed the experimental stage in most agricultural research stations. The use of herbicides for weed control is known and is effective, but specific sensitivity of some spice crops to certain groups of herbicides limits their use. For example, **allspice**, which happily tolerates herbicides derived from urea or from triazine, is very sensitive to the uracil group of chemicals. **Turmeric** is sensitive to 2,4-D while **ginger** tolerates simazine only at the pre-emergence stage. In Australia, diuron is recommended at a rate of 4.5 kg a.i./hectare. Paraquat, an effective herbicide in controlling *Imperata* sp., can only be used with a great deal of care and attention on **ginger** crops since ginger does not tolerate this product well.

In India, herbicide trials have revealed the advantages of using herbicidal treatments based on oxyfluorfen at 0.15 kg a.i/hectare and on oxadiazon at 1 kg a.i./hectare. In trials, this had no residual effects on the groundnut crop which followed **turmeric** in the rotation. It is considered that in most plantations, treatment with herbicides followed by manual weeding is more profitable than two rounds of manual weeding. In a combined crop of turmeric with maize and pigeon pea, spreading LASSO (alachlor) at the pre-emergence stage at a rate of 2 kg a.i./hectare was found to be more economical than all the other treatments tried, including manual weeding.

On **ginger** grown in India, the application of the pre-emergence stage of 2,4-D or atrazine at a rate of 1 kg a.i./hectare gave an equivalent result, in terms of yield, to that of four weeding rounds.

Vanilla, grown between sugar cane in Réunion, appears to be relatively resistant to the herbicides traditionally used for sugar cane. However, during spreading, a guard mounted on the lance of the equipment is essential and the use of herbicides such as 2,4-D or gramoxone, is preferable to that of products which have a long-term residual effect, such as karmex or diuron.

Mulching

This term refers to the act of spreading, on a cultivated plot, a fairly dense layer of a material which is usually, but not necessarily, of vegetable origin. This layer (mulch), which should be as durable as possible, protects the soil from run-off and exposure to the sun, regulates rainfall infiltration, slows down evaporation, arrests or at least considerably restricts weed growth and is generally favourable to growth and yield since it also adds humus to the soil on decomposition.

Mulching is used on many of the species studied and is applied in various ways. Mulching of **vanilla** is carried out as soon as possible after planting. A mixture of grasses and leguminous species is recommended. On Réunion, decomposed bagasse gives good results provided that:

- the bagasse used is at least one year old;
- the bagasse does not come into contact with the vanilla plants. If this happens, it can lead to rotting of the plants.

If spread according to the above recommendations, the layer may be as much as 10 to 20 cm thick in order to be of the greatest benefit to the vanilla plant.

In **pepper** growing, mulching is very widely used in intensive cultivation. Fragments of either vegetable material of various origin or plants grown specifically for this purpose are used. If mulching is carried out correctly, large quantities of mulch will be required, approximately 25 to 30 kg/plant, i.e. 60 to 75 tonnes for 2500 plants/hectare! In Kampuchea, a very widespread local weed, Laos grass (*Eupatorium odoratum*), was frequently used. However, one solution to the problem of providing material is to grow a crop solely for supplying mulch. One such plant which grows rapidly and which in good soils can supply 150 tonnes of living material/hectare/year is *Tithonia diversifolia*.

In Brazil, in the Altamira region in the state of Para, a relatively light mulching of 3 tonnes/hectare of rice husks, hay and sawdust has resulted in a doubling of the yield when compared with an unmulched control.

Various materials have been tested locally for mulching **ginger** in India and Pakistan: mango leaves, rice husks, sawdust, either alone or mixed with sand. In a trial carried out in the state of Bihar in India, the yield of the control was awarded a rating of 100 while the plot which had been mulched with dry leaves and straw was awarded a rating of 172. In the state of Kerala (Malabar, India), mulching is traditional. A first mulching of green leaves is applied to the plantation at a rate of 4 to 9 tonnes/hectare, a second is applied six to seven weeks later, when the **ginger** plants really start to develop and a third mulching is carried out six weeks later. In other areas, mulching is often less carefully carried out and is generally applied only once. Mulching has also been shown to have a positive effect on the growth and yield of **turmeric** in India.

Mulching of **turmeric** is often carried out in India using leaves which have fallen from the shade trees which have been established, since they are necessary for acceptable growth, unless the plantation is in a forest environment. The quantity of leaves used is around 10 tonnes/hectare of dry leaves per year.

> *Mulching is an excellent practice which, particularly for pepper and vanilla crops, should be used more widely in small family plantations.*

Supports, training and shading

This section relates only to the climbing species, except where shading techniques are involved.

Non-living supports

The use of non-living supports, which consist of pieces of wood or other materials, is a practice which, theoretically at least, has many advantages. Support for the vine can immediately be placed where it is required; it

Fig 14   *Mature plantation on non-living supports. Athane Boue, Gabon (Larcher)*

does not compete with the crop in any way, nor does it need to be maintained, and is capable of lasting for a long time if the material selected is suitable.

In reality, even with hard woods, non-living supports rarely last for more than ten years under tropical conditions. They are susceptible mainly to termite and fungal attack, particularly the part of the support which is below ground level. These non-living supports are stakes, 3–5 m high in the case of the **pepper** plant, with a diameter of 10 to 15 cm (Fig 15). Before being put in place, the parts to be inserted in the ground (approximately one quarter of the total length) are treated with preservatives. They may be coated with tar, coaltar or even painted. A simple precaution is to burn the end of the stake. Soaking in a copper sulphate solution, Bordeaux mixture or in other fungicidal or insecticidal products has also been recommended. It is difficult to assess the true efficacy of all these treatments; the main factor being the type and quality of wood used.

The use of solid, squared hardwood sections approximately 10 cm × 10 cm gives good results, but timber is expensive. Reinforced concrete stakes have been tested. **Black pepper** attaches itself well to the surface of concrete, provided that, when the stakes are manufactured, the mould gives the concrete a furrowed and granular surface. Here too the results are fairly satisfactory, but the cost is generally too high. Training the plant on trellises similar to those used for grape vines, i.e. vertical stakes connected by wires forming espaliers, is not suitable for the **pepper plant**. The vine does not climb well on wire, hence a reduction occurs in the growth of the plagiotropic branches, resulting in a fall in production.

Fig 15 *Mature pepper plants on non-living supports. Athane Boue, Gabon (Larcher)*

Living supports

Vines, in particular **vanilla**, are most often grown on living supports; the number of botanical species used as supports being fairly high. It is necessary, first of all, to select species which are themselves of economic importance. This then becomes a true mixed crop (see 3.3 Cultivation systems, page 30).

This is particularly true for **pepper** planted in coffee and tea plantations which are shaded by trees. The pepper plants use the shade trees as supports or may even climb on the trunks of the main crop. Coconut palms, areca palms, rubber, oil palms and even breadfruit trees or ylang-ylang may also provide suitable supports. In this system, **pepper** cultivation must be secondary to the requirements of the main crop and tolerate any disadvantageous factors such as excessive shade, unfavourable nature of the bark and competition at root level (Fig 16).

With species which have no other function than to act as a support, the following qualities can be specified:

• hardiness, resistance to pruning and trimming;

Fig 16 *Pepper vines on* Dracaena *sp.. Petit Okana plantation, Gabon (Larcher)*

- deep rooting, with the taproot not impeding the root system of the vine;
- ease of propagation and planting;
- general morphology and quality of the bark allowing effective attachment, therefore enabling the vine to climb freely;
- selection of species which belong to the leguminous plant family. This is preferable, but not essential.

In India, *Erythrina* spp., leguminous plants with magnificent red flowers, are used for **pepper**, in particular *E. indica* and *E. lithosperma*. In Kampuchea, *Leucaena leucocephala* and *Cassia siamea* are used, and both *Pterocarpus* sp. (Sandragon) and *Gliricidia maculata* (also used as a support for vanilla) are used in Madagascar. In the Central African Republic, several species have been tested, with preference initially being given to those selected from the local flora. However, in the final analysis, *Leucaena leucocephala* and *Melia azedarach* (Persian lilac) proved to be the most suitable.

In Madagascar, *Melia azedarach* has proved to be a good support, but trials have also revealed the suitability of rubber (*Hevea brasiliensis*) not used for latex collection.

In the vanilla plantations of Réunion, the living support *Gliricidia maculata* has proved to be better than all other species used including pignon (*Jatropha curcas*), filao (*Casuarina equisetifolia*) and mulberry. *Gliricidia* is propagated from large cuttings, 1.2 m long, taken from lignified wood two years old. The cuttings are inserted directly in their final positions. The soil is earthed up at the base of the plant and care is taken to avoid a trough forming around it, as stagnant water could kill the cutting.

In the Seychelles, shortly after the end of the second world war, **cinnamon** was used as a support for **vanilla**. Cinnamon, which was planted in the form of large cuttings 4–5 cm in diameter, rooted easily in the climate of these islands.

Living supports need to be pruned. With *Dracaena marginata*, known in Réunion by the name 'candle wood', pruning generally takes place once a year to form high forks so as to allow 'looping' of **vanilla** (see page 59). In addition to normal pruning it may become necessary to prune back excessively high branches which could cause the vine-support combination to sway too much in high winds such as cyclones.

Pepper supports, particularly *Leucaena leucocephala*, are trimmed to reduce the shade and provide nutrients for the soil in the form of a mulch as the leaves and branches decay.

Shading

In **pepper** or **vanilla** plantations provided with living supports, adjusting the shading is linked with correct pruning of the supports, a task which requires care and attention. In the first year, it is enough to prune the lateral branches so as to obtain a sufficiently high single trunk. Further growth in height is then prevented by topping the tree, which encourages the formation of a canopy but still provides light shade. *Leucaena leucocephala* is very well suited to this approach, as the prunings which are left at the base of the tree provide the soil with nitrogen-rich organic matter.

With **vanilla**, the shading provided by the living support is often inadequate. It can be supplemented by planting a range of shade trees, for example, *Albizzia lebbeck* and *Inga edulis*.

Shading is useful in the early stages of growth for tree species of spice plant. With **cinnamon** and **allspice** it should be reduced later, but with **nutmeg** it can be partly retained up to the age of six or seven years. In Indonesia, some plantations are lightly shaded by *Samania saman*. In Madagascar, shading only appears to be useful for **cloves** at the time of planting. In Tanzania, on the island of Zanzibar, vegetative growth has been seen to improve under shade but with a corresponding reduction in yield.

For members of the Zingiberaceae, such as **ginger** and **turmeric**, the question of shading does not arise. It is clear, however, that in mixed crops, the shading provided by the associated crop can be beneficial (Fig 17). For example, in a trial carried out in Bangladesh on a mixed crop of **ginger** and gumbo (okra), it was found that the rhizomes of ginger produced under temporary shading afforded by the gumbo were heavier and larger than those of plants which had not been shaded. **Cardamom**,

Fig 17   *Ginger plants under shade. Anjouan, Comoro Islands (Larcher)*

which is indigenous to a forest micro-climate, yields more and grows better under shade. In India, the forest canopy is retained but is thinned out in stages. In the State of Kerala, trials on various shade tree plantations have shown that *Diospyros ebenum* is an effective shade tree. Other species such as *Thevetia neriifolia*, the breadfruit tree and the badamier are also useful as shade trees and, at the same time, provide a mulch as their leaves fall.

Melegueta pepper, which is also a shade-loving plant, is grown under natural forest shade in cool, moist soils.

Fertilisers

In spite of the considerable number of fertiliser trials carried out on the various crops discussed in this book, and particularly on **pepper**, a great many uncertainties still remain, as with traditional practices in the area of fertiliser application. There is almost unanimous agreement on the advantages of using organic fertilisers to which the effective action of mulching is linked; but if the various elements of mineral fertilisers are examined one by one, as they are below, it is often difficult to determine any clear pattern, except for some of the Zingiberaceae which, since they are grown as annual crops, react more directly to fertilisers, at least in terms of the mass of dry matter produced.

Nitrogen

Annual rates of application of nitrogen recommended for the mature **pepper plant** range from 100 to 200 kg N/hectare/year, preferably in two applications. The fertiliser is spread in a circle around the base of each vine. The doses of nitrogen applied in India to **ginger** and **turmeric** vary between 50 and 100 kg/hectare/year, preferably in several applications. **Ginger** crops in Queensland, Australia, currently receive far more, around 300 kg/hectare/year. During trials with increasing application rates, from 56 to 896 kg N/hectare/year, the optimum rate was found to be between 200 and 300 kg N/hectare/year. In addition for all rates of application, the degree of branching on the rhizomes harvested (the hands) had increased. These high rates of nitrogen application are split as follows: 8 per cent on planting, and the remainder in equal parts after each harvest.

For **cardamom**, the levels of nitrogen applied in India vary between 30 and 50 kg/hectare. It is generally recommended that nitrogen should be applied in two applications, in May–June and September–October.

Phosphorus

Recommendations regarding the levels of application of this element vary far more than they do for nitrogen. Consequently, the levels for **pepper** in India vary betwen 25 and 50 kg P_2O_5/hectare/year, whereas in Brazil, between 200 and 300 kg/hectare/year is recommended.

For most species of Zingiberaceae, between 35 and 60 kg P_2O_5/hectare/year is considered to be appropriate, but often this has no apparent effect.

Potassium
In India, the quantity of K_2O applied annually to pepper is similar to that for nitrogen, i.e. 100 to 200 kg. In Brazil it is higher, around 250 kg. For the Zingiberaceae, the application rates of K_2 and N are comparable. In Australia, three applications of 20 per cent, 40 per cent and 40 per cent of the total dose have been found to be more effective.

Lime and magnesium
Little information is available on the effectiveness of these elements. It should however be pointed out that previous recommendations for liming **ginger** plantations in Australia have been completely abandoned in the light of recent experiments which have shown that the calcium requirements of ginger are very low.

Trace elements
Manganese is toxic to **pepper**. Zinc deficiency in **turmeric**, which occurs particularly on chalky soils, reduces yield.

Organic fertilisers
On Réunion it is considered that mineral fertilisers are of little advantage to the **vanilla** plant whereas mulching is very beneficial. Organic manures are also widely used for **pepper** where, in areas of intensive cultivation, cow dung or other less well-known manures are traditionally used. Thus in Sarawak, Indonesia, bat guano, having as a percentage of total dry weight, 6 per cent N and 8 per cent P_2O_5, or shrimp waste (4 per cent N as a percentage dry weight) is used. Fish waste is also used in Vietnam and Kampuchea. It has already been mentioned that the mulch used in **ginger** or **turmeric** cultivation also represents a considerable supply of organic matter which decomposes after a few months.

It is common practice for **cinnamon**, **nutmeg**, **allspice** and **cloves** to receive little or no fertiliser as mature plants. The Departments of Agriculture recommend various NPK formulae, although research centre trials are not, as yet, very conclusive. In India, in Kerala State, for example, the fertilisers recommended for productive **clove** trees i.e. trees approximately ten years old are 300 g N, 250 g P_2O_5 and 75 g K_2O per tree per year. For a fifteen year old **nutmeg** tree, the recommended application is 500 g N, 200 g P_2O_5 and 1000 g K_2O.

In Queensland, Australia, where **ginger** cultivation is on an intensive scale, up to 11 tonnes/hectare of poultry manure or 175 tonnes/hectare of sugar-cane residues are used. These are obviously very large quantities.

> *The mineral fertiliser formulae recommended for spices vary according to the species and growing sites; their effectiveness and their profitability are not always guaranteed. On the other hand, organic manures, compost or other humus-rich materials are almost always beneficial.*

Pruning and associated operations

This is not applicable to the Zingiberaceae and is mainly of benefit to **pepper**, and, to a lesser extent, **vanilla**. Formative pruning is, however, carried out during the early growth period of some of the species studied here. **Cinnamon**, which in the wild is a tree between 10 and 15 m high, is pruned to obtain a tree with many stems. To achieve this shape, it is cut back to a few centimetres from the ground at around the age of 2 to 3 years. Only four to six shoots are then retained, among the many which grow from the stump; the surplus shoots being cut away carefully to leave the straightest stems possible. These stems are pruned back when they are 2 to 3 m long and 1 to 5 cm in diameter to promote lateral branch production.

Radical pruning of **cloves**, carried out to facilitate leaf plucking (for distillation) often gives disastrous results. It is recommended that systematic pruning should be avoided and that it is sufficient to prune only stems broken accidentally by the winds or the harvesters. **Nutmeg** is not pruned at all.

Pruning, removing inflorescences and tying plants to their supports are important tasks in improving the yield of a **pepper** plantation. The first task consists of tying the vine to its support in such a way that the adventitious roots present at each node of the orthotropic shoots can adhere to the support. The vine must be tied at each node but care must be taken to ensure that it is not pulled too tightly. The upward growth of the vine must be limited to avoid the base being denuded of shoots and also to give strength to the stem. Successive topping operations are therefore carried out. In Kampuchea, the first topping is carried out between 18 months and 2 years, reducing the plant to a height of 30 cm from the ground. Cut in this way, the stem produces a large number of shoots, about ten of which are retained.

In later years, these stems should be tied to the supports in the manner already described. It will then be sufficient to prune the top of all the stems to 4 m. Care must be taken to prevent the tips of the stems, which have reached and overtaken the tops of the support, from hanging down.

A large percentage of inflorescences are removed during the early years of growth. In theory, all the flowers should be removed in the first two years, with two thirds being removed in the third year, one third in the fourth year and none in the fifth year. This practice of removing the inflorescences is also often used to promote maximum production at a specific time by removing all the inflorescences which appear outside a given period of the year.

In **vanilla**, where hand pollination is used, only a certain number of flowers per inflorescence (approximately 12) are fertilised, for the reasons given above.

Selective inflorescence-removal in some **pepper** plantations in Sarawak is aimed at promoting the development of the fruit-bearing branches. This is a relatively complicated technique which should be reserved for plantations where intensive cultivation systems are followed.

The so-called 'looping' operation is peculiar to **vanilla**. It consists of unhooking and carefully detaching the vine from its support using great care in order to damage the adventitious roots as little as possible, passing it through a fork on the support to form a 'loop' with the remaining part of the vine and then retying the vine to the support (Fig 18). The lowest part of the loop may be allowed to come into contact with the ground where plants are grown in a moderately humid environment. In a very humid environment however, such as dense forest shade, contact with the soil should be avoided to prevent any risk of rotting.

Fig 18   *Vanilla plant fruiting (the stem has been 'looped') (IRAT photographic library)*

'Looping' has the advantage of keeping the vanilla plant at a height suitable for harvesting, of encouraging the formation of new shoots and of improving fruiting. In a well-aerated environment, the portion of the loop which touches the ground produces adventitious roots, which help to feed the vine. On well-developed vines two 'loops' can be formed in one year. The vine is attached to its support with the aid of loose ties of vegetable material. Plastic ties commonly used in horticulture, whether sheathed or not, are never used since they damage the vines.

Irrigation

The irrigation practices discussed in this paragraph refer to irrigation of crops growing in their permanent sites and not to the nurseries, in which irrigation is always used.

In the ten cultivated species described in this manual, irrigation is not frequently used and is only carried out, and then rarely, for **ginger**, **turmeric**, and, in some cases, for **pepper**.

Ginger
Irrigation is sometimes used in small-scale garden plantations, where it is treated as a vegetable crop. This is the case in Japan. Where rainfall is inadequate, however, irrigation enables yields to be maintained. In India in 1985, in a research station in Orissa state, reports were published of irrigated plots producing 22.5 tonnes/hectare compared with 11.9 for the controls. In South Africa in 1986, plots were sprayed for 2 hours a day in order to lower the air temperature rather than to irrigate the crop. It was noted that the sprayed plots produced 45.2 tonnes/hectare compared with 36.4 tonnes/hectare for the control plots.

In Australia, irrigation is carried out for two reasons: to compensate for any rainfall deficiencies and to cool the young shoots and protect them from being scorched by the sun. Irrigation is via overhead spray-lines, using a moderate flow rate equivalent to 2.5 mm of rain/hour and must be carried out with great care.

Turmeric
Furrow irrigation is used in the Kerala State of India, on small-scale garden plots and also on mixed crops of turmeric and haricot beans, or onions, coriander or radishes.

Artificial pollination

This technique, which is not very common with regard to agricultural crops, applies only to **vanilla**. In Mexico where this orchid originates, the flowers are visited by small bees of the genus *Melipona* or by humming birds attracted by the nectar. These are the main pollinating agents.

If this species of *Melipona* does not exist in countries where vanilla has been introduced, some human involvement is necessary if fertilisation is to take place. In Mexico, hand-pollination is normal practice on large plantations. This technique was discovered almost by chance on Réunion in 1841. It is carried out using a wooden needle or a large cactus spine (Fig 19).

The sequence of operations is as follows:

1. After separating the sepals and the labellum (held under the thumb), the operator raises the lamella (rostellum) which covers the stigma, using the wooden needle;
2. He then presses on the back of the stamen so that the pollen grains which have clumped together are placed in contact with the stigma. This procedure provides the best possible opportunity for fertilisation to occur, but is not always guaranteed to be successful.

In Madagascar and Réunion it is usual for this operation to be carried out in the early hours of the morning, when the air humidity is still high, but not when it is raining. It is mostly women and children who carry out this work, at a rate of 1200 to 1500 pollinations per morning. From 10 to 12 flowers per inflorescence are pollinated, i.e. 100 to 250 flowers per plant. In five to six weeks, the pod reaches its final size.

In southern India (Tamil Nadu), **cardamom** growers are advised to position bee hives in the plantations in order to increase the pollination rate. Observations have shown that 92 per cent of cardamom flowers are pollinated by bees. This method of pollination with man's intervention, is very similar to the procedure adopted for clover or lucerne seed-producing plots in Europe.

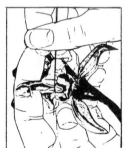

Fig 19 *Artificial pollination of the vanilla plant (after Chalot)*

Vanilla production differs from that of most spice plants in that it requires artificial pollination of the vanilla flowers by hand if effective pollinating insects are absent. Specific skills are required by the workforce for this operation.

---

6 Crop protection

Spice plants can be damaged to varying degrees by living organisms which either enter the tissues of the plant and live there for a period of time at the expense of the host plant, or visibly consume its leaves, stems, flowers or seeds.

These pathogens can be divided into several categories. In practice, a distinction can be drawn between damage due to diseases (viruses, bacteria, fungi) and damage caused by insects, nematodes or other animals.

In the following section, only the diseases and insects which are of practical significance are examined.

6.1 *Diseases*

Bacterial diseases

Bacterial diseases affect:
- **cardamom**: root disease in India due to *Corynebacterium* sp.;
- **ginger**: generalised wilt in Queensland, Australia and also in India and China.

In India, Bacterial Wilt due to *Pseudomonas solanacearum* is considered to be serious, particularly in Kerala State where it appeared in 1978. The recommended treatment is to soak the seedlings in a 0.6 per cent solution of a mercury-based compound for 90 minutes and to rotate the ginger with a non-solanaceous crop.

In Zanzibar, **cloves** are attacked by a serious disease called 'sudden death', which has spectacular symptoms. The foliage of the tree affected wilts from the bottom of the tree upwards. The leaves fall and the tree dies in less than two weeks. This disease was initially attributed to a fungus of the *Valsa* genus. It is now thought, however, that this fungus invades the tissues after the tree has died and the initial causal agent is a bacterium resembling *Rickettsia*. This theory has arisen from studies on the 'Sumatra disease'. This disease, the symptoms of which closely resemble those of 'sudden death', is serious in some parts of Sumatra and in the western part of Java. The disease can be controlled to a certain extent by injections of an antibiotic, oxytetracycline, into the vessels of the wood, but this does not completely eradicate it.

Viruses

Diseases caused by viruses are rare in the range of spice plants studied here. In practice, only one serious disease of this type is described in the literature. This is the virus which attacks **cardamom**. This so-called 'marbling of the young leaves' disease, is of the 'mosaic' type; being referred to as 'Katte' in India. The first symptoms, marbling of the leaves, are followed by stunting of the new shoots, then by the death of the entire bush. The disease is controlled by uprooting and burning the affected plants. In trials carried out at the University of Kerala (India), the disease is being controlled more effectively by treating the plants, before they are uprooted, with an insecticidal solution (0.05 per cent dimethoate) to destroy the aphids which are vectors of the disease. After treatment, the plants are uprooted and burnt three days later. It is advisable not to replant on the same site until two years have passed. With this method, the level of infestation can be kept below 2 per cent. There is, however, a complication. This is the presence of the virus on other plants and in particular on a species belonging to another botanical family: *Maranta arundinacea* (arrowroot), a plant with an edible tuber, grown in India.

There have been reports of 'Katte' in India since 1945. In 1980, in Guatemala, a new species of a mosaic virus was identified on **cardamom**. It is distinct from 'Katte' but causes very similar damage and has the same symptoms. 'Katte' is not of economic importance in Sri Lanka.

Like many other viruses, 'Katte' is propagated, although probably not exclusively, by an aphid: *Pentalonia nigronervosa*.

Cryptogamic diseases

These diseases, caused by a microscopic fungus, are of particular economic importance in **pepper** and **vanilla** plantations, where the damage may be so great that the crop has to be abandoned. For the purposes of this book and also because in many cases the causal agent is the same, these diseases are differentiated according to the part of the plant which is attacked.

Root and collar rots
Several spice species including **cinnamon**, **nutmeg**, **cloves** and **pepper** are found to suffer from root rots similar to those found on many tropical

crops. They are caused by fungi of the genera *Rosellinia, Leptoporus* and *Fomes* among others.

Species of the genera *Pythium, Phytophthora* and *Fusarium* are also responsible for root rot where nematodes are often also involved (see section 6.2). This type of disease is frequently seen in the family Zingiberaceae, but varies considerably in severity. In India, **ginger** rhizomes rotting in the field can cause serious damage and many fungicidal treatments have been tested on them. Products such as zineb (dithane Z–78) and captafol (difolatan) have given good results.

Root diseases of **pepper** and **vanilla** pose particular problems due to their severity.

Vanilla

Vanilla Root Rot, first described in 1917, is found in all the countries in which vanilla is grown and in particular in Madagascar, where it causes serious losses. The disease progresses slowly from the roots, the outer cortex of which becomes cankered. At this stage the disease often goes unnoticed. At a more advanced stage the plant withers, the stems become cinnamon-coloured, the leaves fall and the vine finally dies, sometimes producing only vegetative growth for a number of years. The determination of the causal agent has been the subject of many studies conducted at the research station at Antalaha in Madagascar from 1960 to 1975.

It is clear that two fungal species are responsible: *Fusarium oxysporum f. vanillae* and a *Phytophthora* sp. which is also responsible for mildew damage to the stems, leaves or pods. Correct growing practices, in particular good land drainage and good mulching, have a limited effect on the disease. The solution has been sought (see section 4.1) in the selection of resistant varieties, but few significant results have been obtained so far.

Pepper

Collar Rot, which is widespread in Malaysia and Sumatra and is also called Müller's disease, is due to attack by *Phytophthora palmivora*. The disease often appears after rain. The first symptoms appear on the bark at the base of the stem, the leaves then wither, turn yellow and fall. The affected plants die within a few days or weeks. The leaves which have fallen to the ground are sources of infection for other plants and the disease spreads rapidly. A plantation can be devastated within the space of a few months. Preventive treatment consisting of spraying Bordeaux mixture on the base of the vines and the lower leaves of the plant has proved to be quite effective.

The most reliable form of control, however, is still to use tolerant varieties of **pepper** or preferably those which are resistant to the disease. In Brazil, where pepper growing has increased rapidly since 1950, Root and Collar Rots, with symptoms very similar to those described, have been reported and described since 1964. The disease was then attributed to *Fusarium solani* var. *piperis*. This disease has caused damage so serious that plantations have had to be abandoned. In Bahia state, a *Phytophthora* sp. has been discovered and quarterly treatments with Ridomil (metalaxyl) followed by treatment with a solution of copper oxide (Copper Sandoz) have been recommended. It is probable that, as in the case of vanilla, *Fusarium* and *Phytophthora* spp. are both involved in this disease which, in places, threatens the future of pepper cultivation in Brazil.

> *Collar and Root Diseases in vanilla and pepper plants may become so serious that the crops have to be abandoned.*

Stems

In general, fungal attack on the stems and branches is not very serious. Stripe Canker due to *Phytophthora cinnamomi* has been found on young **cinnamon** trees attacked by *Corticium salmonicolor* (Pink Disease). This can lead to the branches withering, but these attacks have little practical importance. On the other hand, 'die back' or anthracnose can be very serious on **cloves** in Sumatra. Branches withering from the top downwards are the main symptom. The causal agent is *Cryptosporella eugeniae*. As with the damage caused by *Corticium*, it is necessary to prune back the diseased branches to wood which is still healthy, treat the wound with a fungicidal paste and burn all the debris.

Vanilla mildew, which has already been discussed in relation to Root Disease, can attack all the parts of the plant if the conditions are favourable (high humidity). Fungicidal treatments are ineffective and the diseased plants should be uprooted and burnt.

Leaves

Diseases attacking the leaves are normally of no real significance. Fungal infection of the leaves manifests itself in necrosed patches and blight which appears as circular, dark coloured blisters. The genera *Colletotrichum*, *Cercospora*, *Coniothyrium*, *Leptosphaeria*, *Phyllosticta* cause necrotic patches and infection by the genera *Taphrina* and *Exobasidium* takes the form of blight damage. These are the most frequently encountered diseases. Several fungicides have been used and some are effective, but in general no treatment is given. Fungicides may, however, become necessary, for example, for controlling Leaf Galls which infect **pepper**. This disease was reported from the Central African Republic in the 1970s and also occurs in Cameroon. The many galls which form on the young leaves of the most vigorous vines, which are generally those which receive the most sun, are due to the presence of a cryptogam: *Elsinoe piperis*. The effect on yield can be very serious, since the drop in production may reach

Fig 20   Elsinoe piperis *Leaf Gall on pepper grown in Boukoko, Central African Republic (IRAT photographic library)*

60 per cent in severe infestations and 30 per cent in those which are less so. Benomyl treatments are more effective than sprays containing copper compounds (Fig 20).

Flowers, fruits and seeds

Pepper berries have been found to turn black, due to infection by *Colletotrichum piperis* accompanied by *Colletotrichum capsici*. A parasitic algae, *Cephaleuros virescens*, which is also found on the **clove**, may also cause similar damage. These diseases, which are of some significance in Malaysia (Sarawak), can be controlled with fungicides of the carbendazim or benomyl (Benlate) type. 'Pollu', in India, is an anthracnose which also causes blackened berries.

Mildew of **vanilla**, which affects all parts of the vine, can also affect the pods.

In Malaysia and Indonesia, a disease which attacks **nutmeg** develops on the fruit and is caused by *Coryneum myristicae*. The unripe fruits open and release the seeds which are not fully developed and therefore have no commercial value.

In India, cardamom is affected by a disease of the capsules locally called 'Azhukal', due to *Phytophthora nicotianae*. Of the many fungicides which have been used to control the disease, one of the most promising is phenaminosulfan (Bayer 5072).

6.2 Nematodes

Nematodes are a class of unsegmented worms which vary in size. Some are parasites which infest mammals (man in particular), such as thread-worms and *Filaria*. Nematodes which infest spices are very small, visible only under a magnifying glass, and are active in moist, tropical soils where they are very widespread. Some species infest the roots of plants where they cause characteristic deformities such as galls and nodules. Nematode attacks lead directly to retarded growth and production and they also facilitate fungal penetration through the wounds they inflict whilst feeding on the roots.

Most species of nematodes rarely infest a single specific crop. In general, they attack a large number of crops indiscriminately throughout the tropics. Some species which are very commonly found are *Meloidogyne incognita*; *Helicotylenchus* sp.; *Rotylenchus reniformis* and *Radopholus similis*. They are all found on **pepper**, **ginger** and **turmeric**. *Radopholus* causes a great deal of damage to **cardamom** in India and similarly *Helicotylenchus* to **vanilla** in Madagascar. The damage to **pepper** is sometimes so severe that the soil has to be treated. **Ginger** plants are sometimes treated with nematicides before they are planted out. This form of treatment is rare, however, as it is very expensive. In Indonesia and Malaysia, a withering of **pepper** vines occurs and the leaves turn yellow and wilt. This is locally called 'yellow disease' and is attributed to a nematode of the *Radopholus* genus. This is not, however, the only cause with mineral nutrient deficiencies also being involved. A balanced fertiliser application, liming and mulching have been found to control this disease effectively.

In India (Bangalore), clones of **pepper** resistant to nematode are undergoing selection.

It is strongly recommended that **ginger** or **turmeric** crops, which are normally of short duration, are not followed by another crop belonging to the Zingiberaceae the following year. A graminaceous crop, for example a cereal such as sorghum or maize, would be better. Leaving the land to lie fallow considerably reduces nematode infestation. In the Fiji islands for example, it has been noted that shortly after harvesting ginger, the population of *Radopholus similis* is reduced by half and that, six months after harvesting, it is practically nil.

6.3 Insects

The extent of insect damage varies from species to species. In general it is fairly limited and for several of the spice plants dealt with here is insignificant. This is particularly true for **nutmeg**, **allspice** and even **vanilla**. In Sri Lanka, **cinnamon** is rarely attacked but in India there are occasional reports of attacks by caterpillars of the butterfly *Chilasa clytre*, which can cause serious damage to young plantations.

Cloves are occasionally attacked by insects, as happened in Madagascar from 1933 to 1944 when Lepidoptera of a species hitherto unknown, *Chrysotypus caryophyllae*, caused serious damage. The caterpillar excavates galleries which, originating in the smaller branches, advance towards the centre of the tree and the trunk. By manually collecting the caterpillars and chrysalids (more than three million in one year!), infestation was suppressed in 1944 at a time when the absence of insecticides made other methods virtually impossible.

In Kampuchea and Sarawak, Hemipterous larvae of the *Elasmognathus* genus damage the flowers of **pepper**; many flowers fail to develop and often the entire inflorescence may dehisce. This species of *Elasmognathus* is called the 'tiger of the pepper plant' in Kampuchea. In Bangka, another member of the Hemiptera, the 'pepper plant bug', attacks the fruits.

An insect belonging to the Hemiptera (*Nezara viridula*) has also been reported in Réunion and may cause considerable damage to the flower buds and pods. Treatments using bromophos insecticides are effective.

In India, the 'flea beetle' or 'pollu beetle' (*Longitarsis nigripennis*) is responsible for considerable damage to the fruits and may reduce production by 5–20 per cent.

Insects can cause considerable indirect damage to **pepper** by damaging the wooden supports. In India (Kerala), they may also infest *Erythrina* species used as living supports. Due to the galleries which they excavate, these insects weaken the supports which ultimately break. This causes the vines to fall resulting in various types of damage and the need to replace supports and re-attach the vines.

Two types of insect cause significant damage to members of the Zingiberaceae: borers and thrips. The most important borer in India, particularly on **cardamom** and **turmeric**, is *Dichocrocis punctiferalis*, which excavates galleries in the shoots and capsules. Treatment with insecticides such as endosulfan and monocrotophos gives good results in India.

The Thrips genera differ according to the spices, mainly **cardamom**, **turmeric** and **ginger** which they infest, but the insecticides used to control them are fairly similar. Spraying with 0.06 per cent dimethoate gives good results on thrips in **turmeric** in Coimbatore. An 80 per cent protection rate has been achieved on **cardamom** capsules when dusting with methyl parathion or toxaphene or spraying with fenthion.

6.4 Other animals

Snails, in particular Agate snails, can cause damage to the young plants or to the tender parts (buds) of **pepper**, **vanilla** and other plants.

Loan Receipt
Liverpool John Moores University
Library Services

Borrower Name: Al Matrood,Ahmed
Borrower ID: **********5112

Spice plants /
31111 005795057
Due Date: 06/03/2014 23:59

Total Items: 1
13/02/2014 16:48

Please keep your receipt in case of dispute.

Birds can be responsible for serious losses, at the harvesting stage, of some species of spice grown for their fruits, particularly allspice. Fortunately, birds are not attracted to the fruits when they are not completely ripe, and it is at this stage that the fruits are harvested.

When peppercorns are ripe, they are a bright red colour which attracts birds. White pepper or 'bird pepper' is produced as a result of ingestion of ripe peppercorns by birds. After ingestion, the whole red berry passes through the bird's digestive tract, its pulp is completely digested while the seed can be recovered intact in the droppings at the base of the vine. When washed and dried the seeds are known as 'bird pepper', a top-quality white pepper which is a very rare commercial product.

7 Harvesting methods and yields

Given the diversity of the final products and also the great range of growth characteristics of the species being considered, the harvesting techniques used will be dealt with species by species.

7.1 *Pepper*

Pepper is harvested by hand, spike by spike. As the vines are attached to supports 4 to 5 m high, a ladder or step-ladder is used to collect the higher spikes. In general these ladders are made from local materials. They are often very heavy and difficult to handle. Aluminium alloy ladders and step-ladders, although more expensive to buy, last far longer, are far better adapted to the work and are currently the best solution. Harvesting is carried out in various ways depending on the type of pepper to be prepared. For **black pepper**, slightly unripe spikes are harvested, i.e. when most of the berries are yellow but with a few which are red. For **white pepper**, ripe spikes have to be harvested in which at least 75 per cent of the berries are red. For **green pepper**, the spike is harvested when it is still green with no more than 10 per cent of yellow berries. In all cases, several picking rounds will be necessary during the harvesting season.

7.2 *Vanilla*

Ladders and step-ladders are needed for this plant also, in order to harvest those pods which are out of reach.

Frequent harvesting is even more important for vanilla than for pepper. The fruits of vanilla have to be harvested when fully ripe, but before they open in order to obtain a product which, after processing, can be regarded as being of top quality (Fig 21). On Réunion a weekly harvest is carried out during the fruiting period, i.e. a total of about a dozen picking rounds each year.

Fig 21   *Vanilla fruit 'broom' (IRAT photographic library)*

7.3 *Cinnamon*

This species is grown for its bark, commercial cinnamon, and also for
the leaves which are distilled to produce an essential oil which has
different characteristics from that of the essential oil of the bark.

Harvesting the bark

The stems are cut close to the base of the plant and the bark is removed
immediately in a special workshop. The cut stems are 1 to 5 cm in
diameter and 2 to 3 m long. Harvesting is carried out during the rainy
seasons in Sri Lanka when the young leaves appear.

When the leaves and tips have been removed, the bark is removed using special knives with copper alloy as opposed to steel blades. The bark fragments removed are about 30 cm long and are left in a bundle for one night to ferment before the outer corky layer is removed by scraping. The strips of bark obtained in this way then undergo various drying and sorting operations which will be discussed in the next chapter.

Harvesting the leaves

This is mostly limited to self-sown populations of cinnamon plants, the stems of which are not (or no longer) used for bark production. In the Seychelles the leaves are harvested by cutting the stems approximately 20 cm from the ground so that the leaves can be removed easily by hand. The leaves must be distilled immediately to limit essential oil loss as much as possible. Stems which have been stripped of their leaves may then have their bark removed.

7.4 Cloves

Two products of this plant are harvested: the flower buds and the leaves.

Flower buds (cloves)

The stage at which the flower buds are harvested is of great importance. If picked too soon, they wrinkle upon drying and produce cloves which are relatively low in essential oil. If picked too late, the petals and stamens will have fallen, reducing its value.

Because of the size of the trees, ladders are necessary, unless the harvesters are able to climb the trees. This practice is traditional on the island of Zanzibar (Tanzania), but branches are frequently broken in the process. In Madagascar, where light bamboo ladders are used for harvesting, the damage is considerably less and the quality of the harvest relatively good. Cloves also require frequent harvesting.

Leaves

In Madagascar, small branches with the leaves attached are cut for distillation. Planting trees in hedges is helpful in this type of production. Under these conditions, 'clove' production becomes very marginal. Approximately 60 kg of prunings (leaves and branches) have to be distilled to produce 1 kg of essential oil.

In Indonesia, the leaves which have already fallen from the trees are dried in the sun before being distilled.

7.5 Other trees

Allspice

Harvesting the fruit of the allspice plant is not particularly difficult, unless the size of the tree poses a problem. The berries are harvested when still green, as the spicy flavour diminishes with maturity. Unfortunately, and all too often, the fruit-bearing branches are broken off during harvesting and thrown to the ground where another team of workers separate the fruits from the branches. This is carried out by nimble-fingered children and is obviously a very inefficient method since the trees are defoliated. Insects and fungi penetrate the wounds made on the twigs and some of the larger branches. Allspice wood breaks very easily and there is no doubt that this primitive harvesting technique reinforces the biennial bearing tendency of the crop.

Nutmeg

Two different harvesting techniques are used. In Indonesia, the fruits are collected using a device consisting of a small basket fixed to the end of a long pole with a sharp blade. The fruits collected in this way are hardly ripe. In Grenada, only fully ripe fruit which has fallen to the ground is collected. Unripe fruit gives a poor quality product. To avoid any deterioration, it is recommended that a fallen fruit should not be left on the ground for more than 24 hours. Frequent harvesting is therefore essential.

7.6 Seed-bearing Zingiberaceae

Harvesting the capsules of **cardamom** and **melegueta pepper** (Fig 22) is carried out manually. Only the capsules which are ripe but not yet dehiscent are harvested, i.e. at the stage when they are turning from green to yellow. A fully ripe capsule will split open, ejecting its seeds. As the capsules of a single inflorescence on the **cardamom** plant do not all ripen at the same time, the capsules have to be picked one by one, using scissors, retaining a small portion of the stalk.

7.7 Zingiberaceae with rhizomes

Ginger or **turmeric** are harvested using spades or forks to dislodge the clod of earth at the foot of the clump, taking care, as far as possible, not to damage the rhizomes. They are immediately cleaned and the soil

Fig 22   *Fruits of the melegueta pepper plant (IRAT photographic library)*

adhering to them is removed (Fig 23). In Jamaica, they are soaked in water after this preliminary cleaning to make the subsequent stages of preparation easier.

In Australia, a first, preliminary harvesting is carried out approximately six months after planting a slightly or non-fibrous **ginger** for confectionery use. This harvesting is done manually with the rhizomes still firmly adhering to the base of the stems. Normal harvesting at nine months is often carried out mechanically using a suitably adapted or slightly modified potato-lifter.

Fig 23   *Turmeric rhizome (IRAT photographic library)*

Table 9   *Yield/hectare*

Crop	Time between planting out and first harvest (years)	Time between planting out and first good harvest (years)	Average life of the plantation (years)	Yield/hectare
Pepper	3	5	15	Very variable depending on growing method: 350 kg/ha to 3 750 kg/ha of black pepper (India) (Kampuchea)
Vanilla	3	7	10	1 000 to 1 400 kg/ha green pods (Madagascar) 375 to 2 000 kg/ha green pods (Réunion – with sugar cane) 50 to 450 kg/ha green pods (Réunion – grown in woodland)

Crop	Time between planting out and first harvest (years)	Time between planting out and first good harvest (years)	Average life of the plantation (years)	Yield/hectare
Cinnamon	6	6	25	180–220 kg/ha top-grade bark 60–65 kg/ha lower-grade bark
Nutmeg	8–9	16–25	60	800–1 250 kg/ha nutmeg and 200–300 kg/ha mace
Cloves	10	15–20	50 100	160–300 kg dry cloves/ha (Madagascar 100–200 kg) 200–640 kg dry cloves/ha (Java)
Allspice	10	10	50	300–350 kg/ha dry fruit
Cardamom	3 (stock) 5 (plants from seed)	4 6–7	30 30	200 to 1 200 kg/ha fresh capsules; up to 2 000 kg in trials. Yields in Sri Lanka are highest between 10 and 15 years and then fall
Melegueta pepper	3	3–4	10	400–600 kg capsules/ha (Ghana)
Ginger	7–10 months	7–10 months	1	*Fresh* 9 to 11 t/ha (India); 11–15 t/ha (Jamaica); 23 t/ha (Brazil); 36–45 t/ha (South Africa); 95 t/ha (Australia; experimental)
Turmeric	18–21 months	18–21 months	2	*Fresh* 22 to 52 t/ha in India (pure crop); 5.5 t/ha (mixed crop with bananas); 17 t/ha (intercropped with cocunut palms)

> *Spices, which are still relatively expensive foodstuffs, and for which the presentation and qualities are standardised and coded, must be harvested, processed and stored in accordance with the techniques traditionally used for each species.*

7.8 Yields

Table 9 gives an outline of the average yields obtained and the average period between final planting and the onset of production. Except for **ginger** and **turmeric**, which give annual or biennial crops, the spice grower has to be very patient. It is therefore obvious that financing these crops on a large plantation scale must take into account many non-productive years during the early life of the plantation.

8 Processing, storage and preservation

8.1 *Fresh products*

In producing countries, **ginger** rhizomes are often eaten fresh, without any prior preparation. They are sold in this form in the markets as are other roots or tubers such as yams and potatoes. Fresh ginger is also sold in Europe in Asian grocery shops and supermarkets. It will keep for two to three months.

8.2 *Freezing*

This method has been used to a certain extent for ten to fifteen years for maintaining the quality of **pepper** picked unripe, when the peppercorns are still green. This **green pepper**, which is less piquant and less pungent than the **black** and **white peppers**, is now commonly used in cooking and is available at an affordable price. In recent years, **green pepper** has also been on sale in freeze-dried form. It is easier to store than the frozen product but is more expensive.

8.3 *Drying*

This is a common practice for most of the products mentioned in the text; the drying procedures differing slightly according to the commodities involved.

Pepper

If the whole fruit is dried, the result is **black pepper**. The fruit is harvested when yellow.

Trials conducted in the Central African Republic have shown that scalding the spikes before drying, not only is of no advantage, but also considerably reduces the content of the chemical components which are

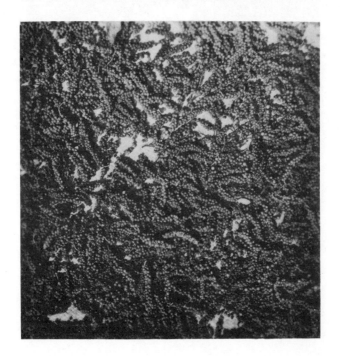

Fig 24   *Spikes of fresh pepper drying. Kampuchea (Marinet)*

important for the berry to develop its aroma. It is therefore recommended that the spikes be dried in piles under shade for 48 hours (Fig 24). The peppercorns should then be removed manually from the spikes and dried in full sunshine in trays; being brought in under shelter at night or in the event of rain. Drying takes from three days to a week. On average, 100 kg of fresh pepper on the spike yields 35 kg of marketable, dry black pepper.

White pepper is the dried peppercorn after the pulp and integument of the fruit have been removed. For this type of preparation, the spikes must be picked when they carry a majority of red, ripe, berries. The spikes are placed in sacks. These sacks are then immersed in running water and left there for seven to ten days. The spikes are then rubbed between the hands in running water which carries away all the debris, hollow seeds and stalks. The peppercorns obtained are dried in the sun for two to three days and are then off-white. On average, 100 kg of fresh pepper spikes yield 21 to 25 kg of white pepper. In India and Kampuchea, **white pepper** is commonly prepared from **black pepper**, as opposed to fresh spikes. The same method, however, is used in the preparation (**Fig** 25). The **white pepper** is then separated from the debris by treading it with bare feet. It is then sun-dried. Under these conditions, 100 kg of

Fig 25 *Black pepper in sacks. Kampuchea (Marinet)*

black pepper yield approximately 70 kg of white pepper. Stagnant water must not be used to steep the pepper, whether fresh berries or black pepper is involved, as this affects the final colour of the product and may also affect the flavour.

Cinnamon

After the corky, outer layer of the bark has been scraped off, this is dried, either in the sun or by artificial means. If sun-dried, plaited mats are used on which the bark strips are laid; these being placed on concrete drying floors during the day and brought in again at night. Sun-drying takes three to five days. Artificial drying takes place in a closed hangar, often heated by burning coconut husks as in the Seychelles. The air temperature in the hangar reaches 60–70°C. Drying is complete after 20 hours.

After drying, the edges of the bark sections curl inwards, giving them the appearance of small tubes. They are sorted for quality and are then traditionally packed into 'quills' by inserting smaller tubes cut with scissors into larger tubes.

Nutmeg

The aril or 'mace' is separated from the seed by hand immediately after harvesting. In Indonesia, the mace is sun-dried on trays for four to five hours a day for two weeks, during which time its colour changes from bright orange red to yellow.

In Grenada, the drying time in the sun is shorter (three days), but the mace is treated periodically by fumigation with carbon bisulphite.

In Indonesia, the seeds are dried in the sun for several weeks and the kernel is then extracted by breaking the thin shell with a mallet. The kernel is often treated by immersing it in milk of lime.

In Grenada, the seeds are dried in the shade in layers under shelters; the layers of seeds being agitated two or three times a day. The kernels are only removed from the seeds when they are required for shipment.

Cloves

The peduncles are initially separated from the flower buds by hand and the fresh cloves and peduncles are dried separately. The cloves are dried in the sun, on mats on a cement floor for two to three days, continuously if possible. Drying under shade gives a less attractive product as does drying which is carried out directly on the cemented floor without mats.

On the island of Zanzibar (Tanzania), where the amount of sunshine during harvesting is less than it is in Madagascar, experiments have been carried out with hot air drying using ovens of the type used for drying copra. The experiments have proved to be successful, provided the temperature is not too high, otherwise the essential oil content will be reduced as it is very volatile.

Allspice or pimento

The berries are dried in the sun, and this presents no particular problems. Hot-air drying is being trialed in Grenada.

Cardamom

Whole fruits are sun-dried on mats, which takes about five days. Some plantations in India also use modified hot-air driers which reduce the drying time to two days. The ultimate aim, in all cases, is to obtain fruits (capsules) which are as white as possible. This is readily achieved when the fruits are dried in the sun in the open air rather than in hot-air driers.

Ginger

The rhizomes of this species are dried to obtain dried ginger, either unpeeled, which gives **coated ginger**. Alternatively, after peeling, washing in water and steeping before drying, **uncoated ginger** or **white ginger** is produced. In all cases, drying takes 48 hours but this varies a great deal according to the climatic conditions and the way in which the layers of rhizomes are turned during the drying process.

Coated ginger is sometimes treated before drying with milk of lime. If treated in this way the ginger is called **bleached ginger**.

Turmeric

The tubers are boiled in water for several hours before being drained and dried in the sun and then ground, since this spice is usually marketed in powdered form.

8.4 *Other preservative treatments*

Pepper

Green pepper is often preserved in vinegar, by a process which is comparable to that used to preserve vegetables such as gherkins and onions.

Ginger

This spice is also found as a **preserve**, which is the traditional, commercial form in China and which is produced almost exclusively in Hong Kong. The ginger is first treated in brine with a high salt content, then steeped in salted vinegar for a week (30 kg of salt + 30 kg of vinegar for 100 kg of ginger which has already been salted). The **salted ginger**, which keeps in good condition for a long time, is used in the preparation of **preserved ginger**, in which a sugar syrup is used as the preservative. In this process, the salted ginger is washed several times, boiled for about ten minutes, then immersed in a heavy sugar syrup (80 kg of sugar per 100 kg of ginger + water), boiled for 45 minutes, left in the syrup for two days, then boiled for a second time for 45 minutes before finally being transferred to the preserving syrup. This preserved ginger is marketed in small barrels (50–100 kg) or in small stoneware pots.

Another popular form is **crystallised ginger** which is prepared in the same way as for preserved ginger, up to the second 45 minute boiling stage. At this stage the ginger is left to steep for a few more days. It is then boiled for a third time until most of the water in the syrup has evaporated. The ginger is then taken out, dried, rolled in crystallised sugar and packed in metal cans.

In general, ginger which is to be preserved is harvested earlier than the dry ginger, i.e. the rhizomes used are younger and less fibrous and they have a looser structure and a less piquant flavour but are more succulent.

Vanilla

This spice is prepared in such a way as to improve the aroma, give the pods an attractive appearance (very dark brown, no splits) and improve their keeping qualities. In Madagascar, the sequence of operations used after harvesting to achieve this is:
- grading into pods of the same length;
- 'scalding', i.e. steeping in hot water at 65°C for one to three minutes to kill the tissues and encourage fermentation to begin;
- 'sweating', a form of fermentation which consists of placing the still hot, barely drained pods into wooden crates, lined with woollen blankets, where they remain for one day at a temperature of around 50°C;
- exposure to the sun on a blanket for three to four days;
- drying in the shade on mats for two to three months;
- placing in 'trunks' for several months during which time the aroma develops. This fermentation period may last for six months;
- final sorting and grading.

This theoretical description of the operation does not take into account the fact that a significant level of skill is required on the part of the operator, who may decide that scalding or sweating should be repeated and may also vary the duration of operations if it is considered to be necessary for good fermentation.

This traditional procedure was considerably improved when hot-air drying replaced sun-drying on blankets. Hot-air ovens are used of the type used to dry prunes in the south-west of France. This method is also used in Réunion.

Another 'revolutionary method' is the preparation of vanilla in 2 to 3 cm sections for the American market which does not favour the traditional presentation in pods and has different standard quality classifications. Indeed, in the USA, a very large proportion of these pods are ground on arrival so that extracts can be prepared. This method means that a finished product can be obtained in around 40 days (8 to 10 days for drying, 30 days for refining), which is relatively cheap since almost all the labour costs have been removed. However, the introduction of this procedure could present a definite problem from the social point of view because in the large vanilla-producing region in Madagascar

(Antahla), most of the population whose livelihoods depend on vanilla preparation would find themselves out of work.

8.5 *Protection of the stored products*

This is only important for **ginger** and **turmeric**, which are normally dried and are therefore more vulnerable to insect attack. The presence of aromatic products in the tissues of most species is probably repellent to insects. Furthermore, the treatments which the products undergo after harvesting, which almost always include prolonged sun or artificial drying, often preceded by hot water treatments and sometimes followed by liming, also contribute towards obtaining a healthy product at the time of packing. Packing is usually done very carefully as is traditional in a trade of this type of commodity due to the relatively high value per kilo. The care taken in the packing operation is a further reason for the successful preservation of the products.

9 Labour requirements

9.1 *Pepper*

Little information is available on this subject. The figures in Table 10 should therefore be taken as a broad indication. The unit adopted is the working day (8 hours/hectare).

In the Central African Republic (according to Larcher), a traditional plantation requires 900 days/hectare to manage with 2500 plants per hectare; a forested plantation takes 83 days/hectare, with approximately 2 000 plants per hectare.

9.2 *Vanilla*

The following information (according to BDPA) shows labour requirements recorded in Madagascar with the units being the working day (8 hours/hectare).

Land clearance	15
Staking out	3.5
Supports	10
Planting the cuttings	15
	———
Total for establishment of plantation	43.5
Weeding	40
Pruning vines	12.5
Pruning living supports	4
Hand pollination	12.5
	———
Total for maintenance	69

(*Continued on page 87.*)

Table 10 *Pepper (after BDPA op. cit.)*

Growing methods	Madagascar Living supports	Zaire	Vietnam Intensive Non-living supports	India Intensive Living supports	New Hebrides
Preparation work	298	200	1 305.5	40.5	112
• manure application	6		213.5		40
• shading		287	63		8
• supports			147	33.5	80
• staking out and hole preparation		100–125			16
Total	304	587–612	1 729	74	256
• cuttings	60	16			
• planting	145	38.5	42		
• maintenance	200	80			
• watering		104	129.5		
• vine tying			224	8	
• Manure application and phytosanitary control			7	25	128
Total in first year	405	238.5	402.5	33	128
• replacements	60				
• maintenance	320			58	200
• manure application and phytosanitary control	6			16.5	128
• vine tying					
Total in second year	386			74.5	328
• maintenance	650			58	200
• vine tying				8	
• trimming supports	6			25	
• manure application and phytosanitary control					48
Total in third year	656			91	248
Total in fourth year	656			91	168
Total in fifth year	656			91	128
Harvest in fifth year	30 kg/day			36 to 75 kg/day	120 kg/day

Harvesting	8
Preliminary drying	5
Transportation	2.5

Total for harvesting	15.5

Overall total	**126**

This total of 126 days should be compared with the gross total of 700 days given for Polynesia. It is apparent, therefore, that as for **pepper**, there are very large differences between one country and another and even between one site and another in the same country.

A detailed study of labour requirements was made on Réunion (Fabre) based on the growing conditions described earlier for vanilla mixed with sugar cane (see page 32), i.e. for a population of 2 500 plants/hectare on living supports. The breakdown is illustrated by Table 11.

Table 11   *Vanilla*

Year			
0	Harrowing – 4 h with a tractor + 15 d or	30–35 d	67–75 d
	Preparing supports and planting out	12–15 d	
	Preparing and planting vanilla	25 d	
1	Replacements	5 d	35 d
	'Looping'	10 d	
	Weeding, tying and second looping	20 d	
3	Looping	20 d	2 h/d for 3 months)
	Pollinating some of the flowers, ringweeding the clumps	15 d	35 d
4	Looping	30 d	205 d
	Harvesting	10 d	
	Cleaning + cutting the tubes	20 d	
	Weeding, looping	70 d	
	Fertilisation	75 d	

h = hours; d = days

N.B. The working days spent on pollination are brought up to 8 hours, i.e. 4 rounds of 2 hours = 1 day's work.

9.3 *Cloves*

The following information (after J. Maistre) shows labour requirements recorded in Madagascar (east coast) with the units being the working day (8 hours/hectare).

Undergrowth clearing	15
Staking out	5
Planting, hole preparation	10
Planting	8
	—
Total	**38**

Weeding
(young plantations)

4×5		= 20
(adult plantations)		
2×5		= 10

Harvesting 25 kg fresh cloves/day,
i.e. 4 to 12 days/hectare.

10 Chemical composition

10.1 *General outline*

All vegetable products contain proteins, lipids, carbohydrates including starch and cellulose and various mineral compounds. Spices, being vegetable products, contain all these categories of substances but also contain fractions which are not present in all vegetable products and which give them their specific characteristics as spices. Many of these compounds are included under the general term **essential oils**. They give the spices their flavour, aroma and smell.

Other chemical substances are also responsible for flavour, for example, piperine which imparts the piquant flavour to the peppercorn. This distinction must not be taken to be absolutely definitive. A spice owes its flavour to a complex mix of simultaneous stimulations of the sensitive nerve endings of the nose and tongue.

The **essential oils** are extracted by distillation with water vapour in a still. The vapour, which is a mixture of water and essential oil, is condensed and collected in a special container designed in such a way that the supernatant fraction can be extracted. This fraction is the **essential oil** of the spice under consideration. Another method of treatment allows other flavour compounds to be extracted, as well as the essential oils. This involves treating the spice with organic solvents such as acetone or petroleum ether. The solution obtained is then evaporated. The resulting product is called an **oleoresin**. Extraction by alcohol, produces some of the **colours** used in the food industry, although these are not strictly regarded as colouring agents. Table 12 shows the conventional, analytical data of the fresh food product, including the essential oil content (except for vanilla) and some compounds which are peculiar to the spice in question (Miscellaneous column). It must be stressed that these are mean values which hide large variations from one sample to another and also from one bibliographical reference to another.

In this table, the high essential oil content of **cloves** and **mace** and also the high lipid content of **nutmeg** and **mace** should be noted. However, the variations in essential oil contents are very great, as shown in

Table 12 *Chemical composition (g per 100 g) of various spices*

Spices	Water	Proteins	Lipids	Essential oils	Starch + sugars	Cellulose	Ashes	Miscellaneous
Black pepper	11	13	8	1.5	41	14	4.6	Piperine 8
White pepper	11	13	7	1.6	55	7	2.1	Piperine 7
Prepared vanilla	33	4.7	8		19	27	5.4	Vanillin 3
Cinnamon	8	4	2	1.1	25	33	5.5	
Cloves	9	4	8	14	16	8	5.2	
Nutmeg	9	7	33	4.5	27	3	2.5	Myristicine
Mace	9	7	22	10.5	24	4	1.8	Myristicine
Ginger	9	8	3	1.8	49	4	4.7	
Turmeric	10	11	8	2.8	38	9	8	Curcumin
Cardamom	11	10	2	5.3	33	17	7.5	

Table 13. The duration and conditions of storage of the spice have a considerable effect on the essential oil content, as can be seen in Table 14.

Table 13 *Variations in the essential oil contents of various spices (After Pruthi)*

Products	% essential oil	Products	% essential oil
Cardamom	5.0–10.75 6.0– 7.0 6.0– 7.0 8.0–10.15	Mace	7.0 –16.0
		Black pepper	1.5 – 3.5 2.1
		White pepper	2.4 2.0 3.25
Cinnamon (leaves)	2.0– 2.05		
Cinnamon (bark)	0.5– 1.0	Green pepper (fresh)	0.9 – 1.5 1.2 – 2.5 1.44– 1.9
Cloves	15.0–18.0		
Ginger	16.0–18.0	Green pepper dry)	2.0 – 8.4 3.6 –10.4 4.6 – 6.9
Nutmeg	1.5– 3.5 5.0– 8.0		
		Turmeric	1.5 – 4.0

Table 14 *Variations in essential oil content of cardamom seeds in Sri Lanka (After Bertile et al)*

Duration and conditions of storage	% essential oil
Seeds extracted immediately after harvesting	4.8
Seeds extracted from capsules stored in ambient conditions for 14 months	2.9
Seeds extracted at harvesting and stored in ambient conditions for 6 weeks	2.4
Seeds extracted at harvesting and stored in ambient conditions for 14 months	1.0

10.2 *Essential oils*

In 10.1 the normal method used for extracting the essential oil from the spices by vapour distillation was described. These essential oils are complex organic products and, in this volume, which is concerned mainly with various aspects of growing spice plants, can be given only basic coverage. Those interested in further details are advised to consult specialist books on organic chemistry.

The essential oils of spices are, in fact, a mixture of various aromatic hydrocarbons and of the oxygenated derivatives of these. The aromatic hydrocarbons belong to a group of cyclic hydrocarbons with a complex structure, called 'terpenes', the structural formula of which is a multiple of 2, 3 or 4 of C_5H_8. A distinction is therefore conventionally drawn between the monoterpenes: $(C_5H_8)^2$, the sesquiterpenes: $(C_5H_8)^3$ and the diterpenes $(C_5H_8)^4$.

The 'C_5H_8', or 'isoprene', group, the expanded formula of which is written: $CH_2=CH-C=CH_2$

$$\underset{\displaystyle CH_3}{|}$$

bonds with itself and polymerises easily since two double bonds between the carbon atoms appear in its formula. For each spice, there are therefore mixtures of terpenes which the specialist chemical laboratories have been trying to identify and assay for almost a century and a half.

Furthermore, the essential oils contain a certain proportion of oxidation products from the hydrocarbons, such as alcohols (ending: '-ol', ketones (ending: '-one') or aldehydes (ending: '-al'). This proportion may become quite large, as shown in Table 15.

Table 15 *Terpene content and content of oxygenated terpene compounds of the essential oils of some spices (After Pruthi)*

Spice	Mono– terpenes	Sesqui– terpenes	Oxygenated compounds
Pepper	**70**	25	5 Piperonal
Ginger	5	**65**	30 Zingiberol, etc
Cardamom	8		**92** Terpineol, etc
Turmeric	10	25	65 Turmerone, etc
Cloves	2	8	**90** Eugenol, etc
Nutmeg	**90**		10 Eugenol, etc
Cinnamon (bark)	10	4	**86** Eugenol, etc

Each spice has its own analytical characteristics; for example, the high proportion of monoterpenes in the essential oil of **pepper** (70 per cent) and **nutmeg** (90 per cent). There is a high proportion of sesquiterpenes in the essential oil of **ginger** (65 per cent), whereas in the essential oils of **turmeric**, **cardamom**, **cloves** and **cinnamon**, the oxygenated compounds constitute the largest fraction.

In cardamom, cloves and cinnamon, as well as in the essential oil of **allspice**, this fraction of oxygenated compounds consists mainly of eugenol.

Table 16 *Physical characteristics of some essential oils of spices (After Fenaroli)*

Physical characteristics	Essential oils of:							
	Pepper corns	Cinnamon bark	Cloves	Allspice berries	Nutmeg	Ginger rhizome	Turmeric rhizome	Cardamom seed
Density at 20°C	0.860 0.904	1.010 1.030	1.044 1.057	1.024 1.055	0.886 0.929	0.872 0.884	0.935	0.919 0.936
Rotatory power	− 8 + 4°	0 − 2°	0 − 1°	0 − 5°	+ 9° + 41°	− 25° − 52°	+ 14°	+ 22° + 41°
Refractive index	1.480 1.502	1.573 1.591	1.528 1.538	1.530 1.540	1.475 1.479	1.487 1.492	1.512	1.462 1.482

These mixtures, the proportions of which vary from one spice to another, are detectable by different aromas and also by different physical properties, as can be seen in Table 16 which illustrates three of the properties normally measured in the laboratory.

The characteristic terpenes have been given names which are generally reminiscent of the plant in which they were first identified. Among the monoterpenes are **pinene** (present in the essential oils of **pepper** and **nutmeg**) and **limonene** (found in the essential oils of **cardamom**); among the sesquiterpenes are **zingiberene** in **ginger**, **turmerene** in **turmeric** and **caryophyllene** in the essential oils of **cloves** and **allspice** (berries and leaves).

The compounds deriving from the hydrocarbons by oxygenation (alcohols, aldehydes and ketones) are very often responsible for the aroma of the spice. Thus, **zingiberol** gives **ginger** its smell; **cinnamon** bark contains **cinnamic aldehyde**; **eugenol** is found in **cloves**, **allspice** and in **cinnamon** leaves. These are a few examples with much simplified chemistry. Although a product of oxygenation usually dominates in a characteristic way in a given essential oil, it is always accompanied by several other compounds in increasingly smaller proportions. These compounds may, however, play a very important role in the formation of the aroma of the oil. An example of this is oil of cloves, in which the methyl amyl acetone content (some fractions of only 1/100th) clearly affects the odour of the oil.

Two of these oxygenated compounds are particularly worthy of note:

- **myristicine**: found in the essential oil of **nutmeg**. This is a toxic compound which, if ingested in too great a quantity, has narcotic effects and may be linked with serious liver disorders;
- **curcumin**: found in the essential oil of turmeric. This is a yellow dye with the structural formula $C_{21}H_{20}O_6$ found in fairly large quantities in the tuber (1.8 to 5.4 per cent of dry weight), together with similar compounds.

10.3 *Other compounds*

Brief references are made in this final section to the nitrogenous compounds present in the tissues of the **peppercorn** and to **vanillin**, an important compound in the formation and aroma of the **vanilla** pod.

Two alkaloids, **piperine** and **chavicine**, are present in all the tissues of the peppercorn, although larger quantities are present in the integument of the seed and in the adjoining pulp.

Piperine (Fig 26) is, in fact, a combination of piperic acid and piperidine ($C_5H_{10}N$), a heterocyclic compound present in many organic substances.

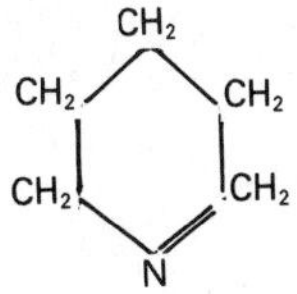

Fig 26   *Piperine*

Piperine is responsible for most of the piquant flavour of pepper. The chavicine isomer of piperine is extremely piquant.

Vanillin is an aldehyde, the expanded formula of which is given in Fig 27,

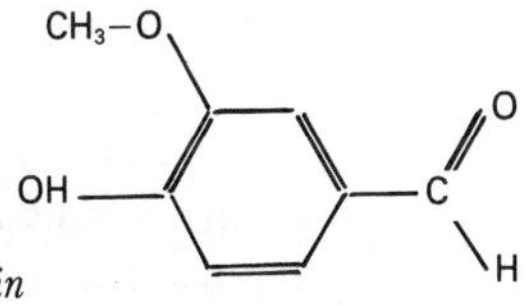

Fig 27   *Vanillin*

and which is easy to convert into piperonal (Fig 28).

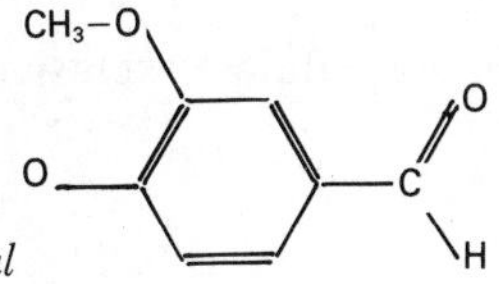

Fig 28   *Piperonal*

Piperonal, like vanillin, is an aromatic compound with a pleasant smell. It is also known as heliotropin and is used in perfumery.

It is relatively simple to manufacture synthetic vanillin from eugenol in industrial chemistry and the sequence of conversion is shown in Fig 29.

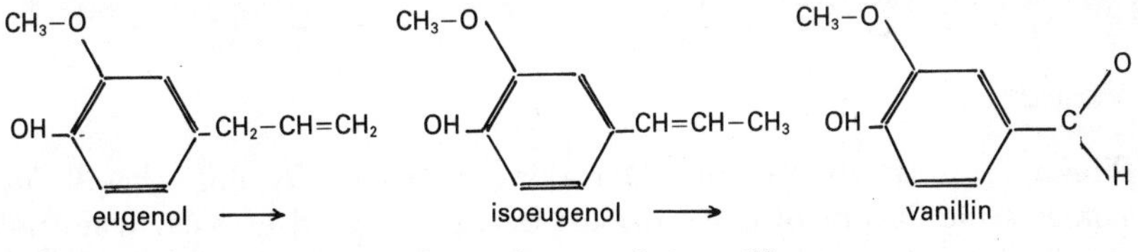

Fig 29   *Sequence of conversion of eugenol into synthetic vanillin*

Eugenol is converted into isoeugenol by being treated with potash; isoeugenol becomes vanillin through oxidation.

95

11 Uses

11.1 *Domestic cooking*

The best known use of spices is in food preparation and cooking. The ten species of spices studied in this volume are used in widely varying amounts, depending on the regions of the world and the culinary traditions of each country. The following descriptions relate to the use of either whole or ground spices.

The essential oils or oleoresins are used almost exclusively by the food industry, except for vanillin.

Pepper

Pepper, in the form of 'black pepper' and 'white pepper', is one of the oldest known spices and has been widely used in Europe since the Middle Ages. Its use in the preparation of meats, venison and fish is well known in many types of cuisine. Only in the Far East (Japan and China) is this spice rarely used. For the past twenty years, 'green pepper' has frequently been used in Western cuisine.

Vanilla

This spice is mainly used in cake-making, confectionery and generally to enhance the flavour of sweet dishes. It is rarely used in Asia. Unfortunately the whole pods are nowadays frequently replaced by extracts or vanilla-flavoured sugar based on synthetic vanillin, even in domestic cooking.

Cinnamon

This species has also been known from ancient times and, as with vanilla, is mainly used in western countries in cake-making, confectionery and in flavouring alcoholic drinks such as punch and mulled wine. In Eastern cuisine, cinnamon is also used in the preparation of meats.

Cloves

Cloves are used in Asia and to a lesser extent in Europe. The clove has a very powerful flavour due to the extremely high essential oil content. In European cuisine it is often sufficient to insert a single clove into one of the vegetables in a dish, whereas Indian and Indonesian cooking use larger quantities. Ground cloves are one of the constituents of curry powder.

Allspice

This spice is popular in traditional American and Anglo-Saxon cooking. It is virtually unknown in Asia and very little used in Europe (with the exception of Britain).

Nutmeg and mace

These are not used to any great extent in Europe, although greater and more regular use is made of them in northern Europe. These spices are used both in cake-making and for flavouring meats and fish cooked in sauces.

Ginger

This spice is used extensively in Indian cuisine and in Far Eastern cuisine in general. In the West it is limited more to sweet dishes. In the English-speaking countries it is added to various alcoholic drinks and ginger ale in particular, which is very popular in Britain and in countries where British culture exists. Crystallised ginger is a sweet in itself.

Turmeric

Turmeric, which is very popular in Indian cuisine, is one of the ingredients of curry powder to which it gives its attractive orange-yellow colour. It is used very little in Western cuisine. It is sometimes used to replace the more expensive saffron in sauces, but the flavour is different.

Cardamom

This spice is little used in America. In Europe too it is rarely used except in Sweden and Finland where its seeds, with their perfumed and piquant flavour, are traditionally used to enhance the flavour of hot alcoholic drinks. In the Middle East, cardamom seeds have been long sought after for flavouring coffee. They are crushed and added to very finely ground coffee. The proportion of cardamom varies between 5 and 50 per cent depending on taste and according to the wealth of the consumer.

Melegueta pepper

Nowadays this spice only reaches Europe sporadically and in small quantities. It is used in the same way as cardamom.

Spice mixtures

These exotic spices are often blended together; one of the best known of these mixtures being curry powder. This is a mixture of various spices ground into a fine powder. The powder usually contains **cloves**, **ginger**, **turmeric**, **allspice**, **cardamom** and **coriander** in variable proportions.

Table 17 *Quantities of various essential oils and oleoresins used in the food industry (in parts*

Foods	Cinnamon bark	Cinnamon leaves	Cloves 'cloves'	Cloves claws	Melegueta pepper	Nutme
Non-alcoholic drinks	6	7	3	59	43	14
Alcoholic drinks			300			
Ice creams	2	3	13	4–7	120	13
Confectionery	80	32	320	91	120	19
Chewing gums	620	160–520	1 800			1–640
Condiments	25	20–78	53	30–70		21
Preserved fruits		3	830			
Meats	50		75 **100**			150
Sweets						
Syrups						10
Pickles						
Soups						
Cakes and pastries	110	50	38	64		75

It may also contain **pepper** and **nutmeg**. Curry powder, which is used a great deal in Indian cuisine, has given its name to the dish which contains it, e.g. 'chicken curry' or 'lamb curry'.

11.2 *Industrial usage*

Food industries use spices in the same form and applying similar techniques to those used in domestic cooking.

Ground or whole peppercorns, cloves and vanilla pods etc. can be used in the pure state. However, in reality, this only occurs in a small percentage of cases. This type of usage is in fact better suited to 'farmhouse' preparations and is often not suitable for mass production where consistent quality is required.

ber million). Oleoresins in bold print (After Fenaroli)

Mace	Black pepper	Allspice berries	Allspice leaves	Ginger	Vanilla	Cardamom seeds
6	3 **59–140**	18	3	17 **79**	**190**	2
		5		20		10
5	0.1–20	15	1	**36–65**	**290**	1
23	12–53	66	34	14 **27**	**210**	6
37		40–1 700	80			2
17 **800**	17 **2 700**	70 **25–130**	80	13 **10–1 000**	**200**	8
33 **100–600**	40 **600**	110 **69**	160	12 **30–250**		36
		29				
35						10–16
	500	55				
68 **360**	8 **450**	48 **600**	32	47 **52**	**300**	57

The food industry therefore tends to use the essential oils or the oleoresins or the two together, rather than the spices themselves. It is easier to keep these products and more convenient to use them because they can be added in very precise measures and mixed in a homogeneous manner. Their flavours are clearly far stronger than those of the spices themselves. For example, on average, the oleoresin of **pepper** has a flavour which is 25 times stronger than pepper itself, and the oleoresin of **ginger** is ten times more powerful than the dry tuber. Table 17 gives an indication of the variety of food products in which spices are used and, additionally, the quantities of essential oil or oleoresin used.

Spices are widely used in cola-based soft drinks which are very popular in the USA, and in lemonades of the 'ginger ale' type which are of English origin.

In alcoholic drinks, spices are used in various 'bitters' and, apparently, in liqueurs such as chartreuse or benedictine, the ingredients of which are closely guarded secrets of the manufacturers. (1) (5)

11.3 *Medicinal uses*

Some of the spices examined in this volume have, in the past, been used in pharmaceuticals and medicines. However, modern medicine makes virtually no use of them now, apart from oil of cloves.

Traditional eastern medicine, however, still commonly makes use of spices for their medicinal properties. Justification for such use is provided by scientific research which has revealed that spices have various capacities among which, according to Pruthi, are:

- **antioxidant capacity**: a property of spices which have simply been ground; more pronounced in aqueous emulsions prepared from these powders. In this form cloves have the strongest antioxidant capacity of all the species tested;
- **preserving capacity**: this is due to the spices inhibiting the growth of micro-organisms. It is caused by the presence of compounds such as eugenol, cinnamic aldehyde and curcumin, which have a preserving action specific to the spices and essential oils. It is also due to the action of the latter on the resistance of the micro-organisms to heat; they break down this resistance;
- **antimicrobial capacity**: in traditional Indian medicine, black pepper, cinnamon, nutmeg, cloves and ginger are used in varying proportions in preparations for various intestinal disorders.

During the 18th and for most of the 19th century, western medicine also used various spices such as **ginger** to improve gastric tone and to facilitate digestion. **Cardamom** also has similar uses.

Nutmeg is used to cure coughs and **black pepper** is used in preparations for promoting sneezing and clearing the airways. Relatively recently, in certain parts of rural France, ground black pepper was sprinkled on bruises or small wounds to promote healing. This practice clearly shows that the antiseptic action of pepper, which has been established scientifically, has been recognised intuitively for a long time.

Cloves were once used in preparations for disorders of the digestive tract, particularly in various 'liquors' or 'elixirs' which have since disappeared from the modern pharmacopoeia. **Oil of cloves**, however, is still frequently used as an effective antiseptic in dental surgery in particular.

The aphrodisiac properties attributed to various spices in some countries are to be regarded with great scepticism. Such properties have never seriously been established but occasionally reappear in the press.

A large number of research laboratories, particularly in the Far East, are carrying out detailed studies on the medicinal properties of many of the spices examined in this volume, particularly the compounds present in the essential oils. In Europe, over the past ten years, there has been growing interest in 'aromatherapy', i.e. treating diseases with extracts from aromatic plants. This opens up interesting possibilities.

11.4 *Miscellaneous uses*

Spices, and more specifically essential oils, are used to a certain extent in perfumery to make a variety of products. As far as the 'top-of-the-range' perfumes are concerned, it is difficult to be specific, given the closely-guarded secrets of their compositions. On the other hand, it is well known that the essential oils of **black pepper**, **cloves** and clove leaves and **allspice** are used in the manufacture of after-shave lotions.

Cinnamon oil is used in some perfumes, but the quantities must be small due to the risk of skin sensitisation. **Turmeric** oil is only used in inexpensive perfumes of the 'oriental' type.

The perfumery industry also uses components of the essential oils, namely eugenol and isoeugenol which are present in several of these. The essential oil of **pepper** contains **piperine**, which after a variety of relatively simple processes gives **piperonal**, which is artificial heliotropin.

In Indonesia, and more particularly in Java, the tobacco in special cigarettes is flavoured with **cloves**. The cloves, which are ground into small fragments (but not powder), are evenly mixed in with the tobacco. These cigarettes, which have a very strong aroma, are very popular with local consumers. This explains why Indonesia is the largest consumer of cloves in the world and has actively encouraged domestic production of the spice being now (1989) virtually self-sufficient.

The main use of the essential oil of **cloves**, however, is in the manufacture of artificial vanillin from eugenol. This constitutes 78 to 98 per cent by weight of the essential oil of cloves. For economic reasons, the essential oil of clove leaves is mainly used for the extraction of eugenol, although the content is a little less (75 to 88 per cent). The essential oil of **allspice** leaves is also used for the extraction of eugenol.

Synthetic vanillin, obtained by simple industrial processes, is a dangerous competitor to vanilla, although, in fact, the aroma and flavour of natural vanilla are more subtle and varied. It is obvious that the vanillin present in the pod is the main agent of the flavour, but it is not the only one and other compounds (see Chapter 10) contribute to the variations in flavour.

Spices were once used for their insect-repellent properties. However, the arrival on the market of an extended range of more effective synthetic products has virtually put an end to this use nowadays.

In the past, for example, **black peppercorns** were used to protect fur garments from moths and other insects. The peppercorns were placed in contact with the fur and the garment was protected by a waterproof paper bag. Seville or ordinary oranges spiked with **cloves** are put in linen cupboards to give a pleasant fragrance to the confined space in the cupboard, but they may, in addition, repel insects to some extent. The essential oil of **cinnamon** is added to some insecticidal powers.

An essential oil can also be extracted from **nutmeg** leaves, either fresh (0.4 to 0.6 per cent) or dried (1.6 per cent). This oil, in which there is no trade, is said to have herbicidal properties.

The fat contained in the **nutmeg** (25 to 40 per cent) is extracted after crushing the kernels and expressing it with steam. It is an orange-coloured fat known by the name of 'nutmeg butter' and is used in the pharmaceutical industry.

The pigment present in the cells of **turmeric** rhizomes, **curcumin**, can be used to dye fabrics and also as a food-colouring agent. Curcumin can be isolated in the form of a crystallised, orange-yellow powder with a melting point of between 180 and 183°C. In India, turmeric itself is used to colour fabrics.

The use of spice plants for medicinal purposes, which is as old as the spices themselves, has, until recently, been gradually disappearing. Current pharmacological research and the development of 'herbal medicines' could give new impetus to this use.

11.5 *Imitations and substitutions*

All the species studied, except for **melegueta pepper**, which is rarely marketed today, have been defined by law and their presentation must adhere to the standards laid down by the regulations. Initially, the texts give the scientific definition of the species in question. In France, for example, only the fruits or seeds of the species *Piper nigrum* can legitimately be called **pepper**, and only the bark of *Cinnamomum verum* can be called **cinnamon**. It would therefore be fraudulent to market food from another species under a common name reserved for a single species, even if the former species was of the same genus.

As well as substitutes of this kind, there is also the kind of fraud which consists of mixing in with the genuine commodity, a certain proportion of the same commodity which has lost its value since the essential oil has already been extracted. This type of fraud exists for **ginger**, **cloves** and **peppercorns**. Commodities which have lost their value can easily be recognised under a binocular magnifying glass, or a microscope. In powdered form, however, they are more difficult, but not impossible, to detect. The more obvious frauds consist of mixing in vegetable material, the botanical origin of which differs enormously. This can also be easily detected under a microscope. Examples of this are black peppercorns being adulterated with juniper berries and vetch seeds.

This problem of similar species being substituted for the species defined by law barely arises for **cloves**, **allspice**, **melegueta pepper**, **ginger** and **turmeric**. It is of little importance if seeds from another species of *Myristica* such as *M. argentea* (Macassar nutmeg) or *M. malabarica* (Bombay nutmeg) are sometimes mixed in with authentic **nutmeg**.

The existence of types of **cinnamon** other than Sri Lankan cinnamon, or 'true cinnamon', complicates matters slightly. In English, all these other types of cinnamon (the quality of which is not as good) are referred to by the name of 'cassia'. This group includes several species of *Cinnamomum*. The main species are *C. cassia* (Chinese cinnamon), *C. loureirii* (Saigon, Annam cinnamon) and *C. burmanii* (cinnamon from Indonesia, Malaysia and Macassar); finally, various *Cinnamomum* sp. make up the 'wild cinnamons' (wild cassia).

The **pepper plant** belongs to a genus with many species, several of which are used as spices, in the same way as is *Piper nigrum*. These other species have a much more limited distribution, since they are rarely consumed outside the area in which they are produced, but they can also be used to adulterate ground black pepper. These species include:

- **'long peppers'**: *Piper officinarum* and *Piper longum*; two species which originated in the Indian archipelago, the first being grown mainly in Indonesia and the second on the western coast of the Indian peninsula (Bengal);
- **'cubeb'** or **'tailed pepper'**: *P. cubeba*; originating in Indonesia and so-named because the base of the peppercorn is slightly extended. It is used locally as a spice;
- **Guinea pepper**: *P. guineense*; fairly common in the tropical forest

and equatorial areas of Africa. The pungency of the dried berry is comparable with that of *P. nigrum*, but the flavour is not the same. This pepper, which is also called 'Kissi pepper' or 'Aschanti pepper', is harvested and marketed.

Some plants which are not botanically related to the *Piper* genus are also called 'false peppers' or 'peppers'. The best known of these belong to the *Schinus* genus of the family Terebinthaceae. *S. molle* is frequently planted in the south of France as an avenue tree. Another species, *S. terebinthifolia*, frequently found on fallow land in Réunion, produces pink berries which turn red on ripening. These berries have a certain popularity in 'nouvelle cuisine' under the name 'pink pepper'. This description, which contravenes the legislation, has now been replaced by the innocuous description 'pink berries'. The flavour of these 'pink berries' is very different from that of true pepper seeds, but is enjoyed by some.

Many species of **vanilla** exist, but only a few are cultivated. *Vanilla fragrans* is by far the most extensively grown. This is 'Bourbon vanilla', characterised by the most aromatic pod, and is the 'vanilla' of commerce.

V. tahitensis, a species of American origin, has a pod which is less rich in vanillin than *V. fragrans* and has a slightly different aroma. The pod is not dehiscent when mature. *V. pompona*, which also originated in Central America and has, for a long time, been grown on Guadeloupe, bears the name 'vanillon'. The pod contains less vanillin than Bourbon vanilla and has a slightly different aroma.

Adulteration rarely affects the whole pods, as the producing countries take care to supply a genuine and standardised product, but more frequently it affects vanilla-based products, some of which are enhanced legally by the addition of synthetic vanillin. This is true for Vanilla essence and Vanilla 'powder'.

The legislation of some countries (with the exception of France and the USA) is clearly inadequate in this respect, and in view of the single market in 1992 it is clearly essential that any ambiguity in the regulations regarding the labelling of edible flavourings should be removed.

A first step has been made in this direction, compelling manufacturers to use the term 'vanillin' instead of vanilla if the flavouring used is vanillin. Further steps have to be taken, adding the words 'natural flavouring' if this refers to vanilla, and 'artificial flavouring' if this refers to synthetic vanillin.

Glossary

Alkaloids Nitrogen-containing organic bases found in certain plants. E.g. morphine in the poppy and nicotine in tobacco. The alkaloids are toxic to the nervous system.

Alluvium Component of soils, the mean particle size of which is between 2 μ and 50 μ in diameter (2 μ to 20 μ: fine alluvia, 20 μ to 50 μ coarse alluvia).

Aril An outgrowth of the integument of certain seeds in the form of a cord or network, near the hilum.

Bagasse The fibrous remains of the sugar cane after the juice has been extracted.

Clone Plants reproduced by vegetative propagation from a common ancestor. All these individuals have the same genetic make-up.

Compost Mixture of organic materials of varied origin (plant debris, household refuse, etc) piled in a heap and having undergone various fermentations transforming them into a product suitable for use as a fertiliser.

Dehiscence Spontaneous opening or splitting of one or more segments of dry fruits (e.g. legume pods) releasing the seeds. The term is also used to describe the opening of anthers to release the pollen.

Dioecism The state of dioecious plants, i.e. those in which some plants only have male flowers and others only have female flowers and therefore subsequently bear the fruits.

Emulsion A liquid of homogeneous appearance containing very fine droplets of another non-miscible substance in suspension, e.g. the fat in milk.

Essence Natural volatile, odoriferous compound extracted from various products by distillation, e.g. the mineral essence extracted by distillation of crude petroleum is 'petrol', used as a fuel in automotives. *See also* 'Essential oil'.

Essential (or volatile) oils Odoriferous volatile organic products extracted by distillation from plant or animal substances.

Fertiliser application Action of improving the fertility of the soil by adding a fertiliser. In current language the term fertiliser application mainly concerns the use of mineral fertilisers.

Freeze-drying Method of preserving food by drying, achieved in the following stages: rapid freezing at low temperatures ($-80°C$) followed by sublimation under vacuum. The flavour is preserved more effectively by this method than it is by drying by evaporation.

Fumigation Disinfecting and, more specifically, insect elimination using gaseous products such as ethylene dibromide.

Fungicide *See* 'Pesticide'.

Glycosides Complex organic compounds capable of being broken down into simple molecules: the sugars. In plants, for example: cellulose and the starches. Alternative term 'carbohydrates.

Graft Bud (scion) or branch of selected material which is grafted onto the rootstock. *See* 'Rootstock'.

Gynostemium Axial organ of the flowers of the Orchidaceae consisting of the union of the style and the median stamen. This stamen has two fertile loculi each containing a **pollinium** (pollen grains united in a small mass).

Herbaceous A plant or part of a plant which has non-lignified tissues which are therefore generally green and tender.

Herbicide *See* 'Pesticide'.

Heterocyclic A chemical compound with a cyclical formula, the 'cyclical' part of which consists of atoms which are not all similar.

Inflorescence Arrangement of the flowers on a common axis which may be either single (spike, bunch, umbel, corymb, capitulum), or branching (cyme, raceme).

Insecticide See 'Pesticide'.

Integument The outermost protective covering of the seed; generally referred to as the 'skin'.

Isomers Substances having the same structural formula, but differing in their expanded formula and having different properties.

Layering Type of vegetative propagation consisting of promoting root development on a part of a branch by covering it with a sleeve containing a suitable medium, or burying it in the ground, separating the branch from the tree only when the roots are sufficiently well developed to enable it to live independently.

Lipids Family of organic compounds resulting from the combination of 'glycerine' with 'fatty acids'. Alternative term: 'fats'.

Manure application Spreading fertilisers and, more generally, organic fertilisers (manure, liquid manure, etc) on the soil to improve its fertility.

Nematicide *See* 'Pesticide'.

Oleoresins Products obtained by treating plants containing essential oils with an organic solvent such as acetone, petroleum ether, hexane, etc. and by evaporating the solvent of the solution obtained.

Orthotropic Branches which grow vertically; in the pepper plant, this type of branch has adventitious roots and gives rise to the 'plagiotropic' branches which bear the flowers and fruits, but it never bears flowers itself.

Pantropical A plant or animal species, the area of distribution of which includes the tropical regions of the four continents.

Persistence Continuation of the action of a pesticide for a longer or shorter time after application.

Pesticide Any product used to combat the enemies of cultivated plants: **fungicide** (against fungi); **herbicide** (against weeds); **insecticide** (against insects) and **nematicide** (against nematodes).

pH Conventional index measuring the degree of acidity of a medium, ranging from 0 (maximum acidity) to 14 (maximum alkalinity); 7 being neutral.

Plagiotropic Branches which grow horizontally. *See* 'Orthotropic'.

Polymerisation Union of a certain number of identical molecules, thus giving rise to a chemical compound with totally different properties. E.g. the rubber polymer of isoprene.

Proteins Nitrogenous compounds; essential components of living matter, formed by the joining together of simpler compounds: the amino acids.

Rootstock Ligneous growth on which grafting is performed.

Rostellum In the flower of the Orchidaceae: extension of the tip of the style into a thin lamella (which is a non-functional stigma).

Rotation Methodic succession of the crops planted on a given area of soil and the periods of letting the land lie fallow. *Syn*: crop succession.

Sand Soil component, the grain sizes of which have a mean diameter ranging from 0.05 mm to 2 mm (0.05 mm–0.2 mm: fine sand; 0.2–2 mm: coarse sand).

Sesqui Prefix meaning 'one and a half', used in chemistry. E.g. a sesquioxide of iron.

Vermiculite Mineral of the mica family. Under the action of heat, this compound becomes dehydrated while greatly increasing in volume. Reduced to particles (after heating) it is used as a growing medium, particularly in horticulture.

Bibliography

References and further reading

General

Maistre, J. (1964) *Les plantes à épices* (Maisonneuve et Larose, Paris)

Baillon, H. (1877) *Histoire des plantes* (Hachette, Paris)

Atal, C.K. and Kapur, B.M. (1982) *Cultivation and utilisation of aromatic plants* (Council of Scientific & Industrial Research, Jammu Tawi)

Hubert, P. (1971–2) *Recueil de fiches techniques d'agriculture spéciale à l'usage des lycées agricoles* (2 vols., BDPA Agence de Madagascar, Tananarive)

Purseglove, J.W., Brown, E.G., Green, C.L., Robbins, S.R.J. (1981) *Spices* (2 vols. Longman, London, New York)

Pruthi, J.S. (1980) *Spices and condiments. Chemistry. Microbiology. Technology* (A/P. London, New York)

Rosengarten, F. (1969) *The book of spices* (Livingston, Wynnewood)

Vandenput, R. (1981) *Les principales cultures en Afrique centrale* (Administration Générale de la Coopération au Développement, Brussels)

Pepper

Gouaut, H. (1974) *Travaux de recherche sur le poivrier* (Summary and assessment 1966–74. Document no. 9. IRAT station, Madagascar. Tananarive)

IRAT. Doc. (1984) *Bibliographie sur le poivrier no. 307 et complément* (Doc./Nogent)

Larcher, J. (1970) *La multiplication du poivrier et l'utilisation des hormones de bouturage* (Agro. Trop., XXV, 9, pp. 746–64)

Larcher, J. (1970) *La culture du poivrier* (Cahier Agr. Prat. Pays chauds, no. 3 and no. 4)

Vanilla

Bouriquet, G. (1954) *Le vanillier et la vanille dans le monde* (Lechevalier, Paris)

Dequaire, J. (1976) *L'amélioration du vanillier à Madagascar* (Journ. Agr. Trop et Bot. Appl. XXIII, no. 7–12, pp. 139–58)

IRAT. Doc. (1987) *Bibliographie sur le vanillier 1724–1986* (NTM/no. 306. Nogent-sur-Marne)

Fabre, C.H. (1987) *La vanille à La Réunion* (Technical bulletin. 85 pp, Saint-Denis)

Chalot, Ch. and Bernard, U. (1914) *Culture et préparation de la vanille* (Agro. Col. Bul. mens. Jardin Col., no. 15–16, p. 95–9)

Cloves

Dufournet, R. (1968) *Le giroflier et sa culture à Madagascar* (Bul. Madagascar, March, no. 262, pp. 216–81)

Ramalanjoana, G. and Jourdan, E. (1962) *L'essence de girofle à Madagascar. Technologie, distillation, emballage* (Agr. Trop., no. 12, pp. 1053–83)

Allspice

Rodriguez, D.W. (1969) *Pimento. A short economic history* (Ministry of Agr. and Fisheries. Commodity bul. no. 3. Kingston, Jamaica)

Ginger, Turmeric, Cardamom

IRAT. Doc. (1988) (Bibliographies NTM 5, 6, 4)

Bertile, W., Michelon, R. and Pieribattesti, J.C. (1980) *Le Cardamome à Sri Lanka (Ceylan). Ses possibilités d'implantation à La Réunion* (Station report, Dept. La Réunion. General council, Saint-Denis)

Melegueta pepper

Van Harten, A.M. (1970) *Melegueta pepper (Aframomum melegueta (Rosc) K. Schumann)* (Economic Botany 24, pp. 208–16)

Lock, J.M., Hall, J.B. and Abbiw, D.K. (1977) *The cultivation of Melegueta pepper (Aframomum melegueta) in Ghana* (Economic Botany 31 (3), pp. 321–30)

Miscellaneous

BDPA (1965) *Techniques rurales en Afrique. 21. Les temps de travaux* (Annex 1, p. 352. Ministère de la Coopération, Paris)

CCI (Centre de Commerce International). Market survey (1986) *Huiles essentielles et oléorésines* (CNUCED/GATT, Geneva)

G. de Geus, J. (1973) *Fertilizer guide for the tropics and subtropics* (Centre for Nitrogen Studies, Zurich)

International Trade Centre UNCTAD/GATT (1982) *Spices: A survey of the world market* (2 vols. CNUCED/GATT, Geneva)

Fenaroli (1971) *Fenaroli's handbook of the flavor ingredients* (The Chemical Rubber Co), Cleveland, USA. Translated and revised by Furia, E.T. and Bellanca, N.

Index

Numbers in *italics* refer to figures or tables where these are separate from their textual reference.

strip weeding 48
substitutes 102–4
supports
    living 53–4
    non-living 51–2

temperature 26, 29–30
terpene content 92, 94
thrips 68
tissue cultures 42
tobacco flavouring 101
trace elements 57
tree spices
    cuttings 42–3
    harvesting 71–3
    morphology 15–20
    propagation 36–7, 42–5
    site preparation 39
turmeric (*Curcuma domestica*) *4, 5, 11*
    chemical composition *90*, 92–5
    drying 82
    harvesting 73–4
    herbicides 49
    intercropping 33
    irrigation 60
    morphology 22–3
    mulching 51
    nitrogen 56
    origins 12
    selection 37
    soils for 27
    spacing *47*
    storage 84
    uses 97
    yield *76*
turmeric rhizome *75*

vanilla (*Vanilla fragrans*) *4, 5, 11*, 104
    artificial pollination 60–1
    chemical composition *90*, 94–5
    and cinnamon 54
    diseases 64, 65, 66

drying 83–4
harvesting 70, *71*
herbicides 50
intercropping 32–3
labour requirements 85, 87
living supports 53, 54
looping 54, 59–60
morphology 14–15
mulching 50
origins 12
propagation 35–6, 39–40
pruning 58
shading 55
soils for 27
spacing *47*
uses 96
weeding 49
yield *75*
vanilla mildew 65, 66
vanillin 94, 95, 101–2, 104
vine spices
    harvesting 70–1
    morphology 13–15
    propagation 34–6, 39–42
    site preparation 38
viruses 63

weeding 48–50
weeds 48
white pepper 70, 79, *90*
wind factor 30

yields *75–6*, 77

zinc 57
Zingiberaceae
    harvesting 73–7
    propagation by rhizomes 45–6
    seed-bearing 73
    shading 55
    weeding 49

Acknowledgements

I would like to take this opportunity to thank the documentation department at the IRAT and, in particular, Madame N. Tran Minh who greatly simplified the documentary problems posed for me in the preparation of this book.

The author and publishers wish to acknowledge, with thanks, the following photographic sources:
IRAT photographic library, and
J. Larcher personal photographic collection.